Ballet

BY ARNOLD L. HASKELL

(A 122)

BALLET

Arnold L. Haskell

WITH EIGHTEEN ILLUSTRATIONS FROM PHOTOGRAPHS

AND TWENTY-FIVE ORIGINAL DECORATIONS IN THE TEXT BY

KAY AMBROSE

BALLET

A Complete Guide To Appreciation

History, Aesthetics
Ballets, Dancers

Arnold L. Haskell

PENGUIN BOOKS
HARMONDSWORTH MIDDLESEX ENGLAND
245 FIFTH AVENUE NEW YORK U.S.A.

First published July 1938
Reprinted July 1938
Reprinted October 1938
Reprinted November 1940
Reprinted May 1943
Revised Edition January 1945
Reprinted 1945

PRINTED IN GREAT BRITAIN IN LETTERPRESS AND GRAVURE FOR
PENGUIN BOOKS LIMITED BY HAZELL, WATSON & VINEY, LTD.,
LONDON AND AYLESBURY

TO

Ninette de Valois

whose artistry, knowledge, inspiring leadership, consistency, and courage have made
the ballet at Sadler's Wells into a national
treasure, and who, by doing so, has added
an exciting new chapter to the history of the
art. And to her company, of the Vic-Wells
Ballet, as she would wish.

A. L. H.

Contents

List of Illustrations

7

List of Illustrations

Introduction to Revised Edition

I HAVE aimed here at a guide to the appreciation of ballet for members of a vastly growing audience and for those dancers and teachers who require a closer understanding of their art, and who realise that steps are not enough.

I have not attempted any technical-mechanical explanations. Such a thing, if at all possible, is intolerably tedious in print and belongs to those who have made it their speciality. There are enough dancing schools to satisfy any wants in that direction. I have included a small glossary of the terms I have been forced to use, purely for purposes of identification. I have tried throughout to avoid any technical jargon.

For the present revised edition I have left the bulk of the text unchanged. This book was conceived as a guide to ballet in general, and the principles laid down cannot date. My main alterations and additions have been in Chapters 6 and 7, which deal with the application of those principles to the contemporary scene. In accordance with that idea, I have included in this edition a series of photographs of our Sadler's Wells Ballet that has grown so greatly in popularity and achievement. This does not mean that Russian Ballet has ceased to occupy a position of importance, and I trust that future editions may have further photographs of Russian visitors to this country, both Soviet and émigré.

I have given a brief review of the war years in an appendix.

I would like to thank Mr. Allen Lane of Penguin Books Ltd. for his interest in the present volume, and for the realisation that in these troubled times an increasing number of people are finding calm in the gentle art of ballet, in which tradition is such a vital factor.

Finally, I would like to thank Miss Kay Ambrose for

placing at my disposal her splendid decorations, which make this little book a thing of beauty.

ARNOLD L. HASKELL.

22 HORNTON STREET, W.8,
  LONDON, 1944.

THE LUNATIC FRINGE

CHAPTER 1

Introductory

The present-day popularity of ballet—Strong influence of the audience—The ignorance of the young dancer—The importance of ballet as an artistic medium—The scheme of the book.

As recently as seven years ago ballet was seasonal, an expensive luxury that appealed to the very few; today [1] in London there is ballet throughout the year, and at Sadler's Wells for a nine-months' season at cinema prices. The art enjoys a popularity it has not known since the middle of last century, if then. In one year, 1936, seven different companies appeared in London, each one performing its version of *Les Sylphides, Carnaval,* and other popular works. Two companies ran simultaneously in the West End, both to good houses. As recently as seven years ago a taste for ballet was considered a trifle precious. There were many jokes about the anæmic-looking, long-haired youths and the short-haired, untidy women in hand-spun fabrics who enthused or muttered the current formula of " What fun, how amusing, my dear." Ballet still has its small lunatic band of hangers-on who make themselves conspicuous both sartorially and vocally, [2] but it has gained a great new public. The man in the street has discovered it and is so enchanted with his discovery that the ballet has become a habit. He has found out that though the repertory of works is strictly limited, the performances themselves vary enormously, and he begins to find a keen pleasure in comparing the various Sylphides he has seen during the past year. Before he knows where he is, he has become a critic.

---

[1] I leave this unaltered. The war has proved that the popularity of ballet was not just a boom.

[2] See Glossary, under *Balletomane,* and illustration, page 10.

It is possible to be carried away by the beauty of ballet, one of the very last strongholds of theatrical illusion, without possessing any critical standards or any backgrounds of knowledge, but only the trained eye will reap the maximum of pleasure from a performance, the man who is conscious, not merely of his enjoyment, but of the reasons behind it.

There are two parties to every theatrical manifestation: the performers and their public; and it is ultimately the public who dictate the quality of the performance. The hypercritical public of the Imperial Russian theatres, those old *habitués* who could count every beat and who could in imagination dance every movement, were responsible for the triumph of a Pavlova.

It was Pavlova who once told the present writer, " The public here is so exceedingly generous that while it warms my heart it does not help me. Tonight, I know that I did not dance the *Dying Swan* as well as usual, but the applause was exactly the same. I would have been pleased if it had been just a little less." Only because she was hypercritical of herself did Pavlova maintain her high standard, and she had learned to be hypercritical from her first audiences in Russia and from the highly evolved system of training that formed her.

Today we are living in an age of rapid results. There is no reason to believe that dancers do not possess the same degree of artistic talent as in the past. Most certainly they have a greater technical aptitude than in former years, but that talent and that aptitude are forced. Where before it took ten years to form a dancer, now it takes three, four, or, exceptionally, five years. More than ever, therefore, the dancer depends upon the critical standards of her audience. But the audience itself is a fresh one that has formed its critical standards from the young dancers. *The need of the dancers and their audience is identical: a background of knowledge that will develop the critical faculties.*

I have tried in this book to prepare such a background, both for the spectator and for the young dancer. No art can be learnt from a book, but a book can help the tyro to sort out his own loose impressions, and to form for himself a basis of criticism that will add, not only to his pleasure, but in the end to the healthy development of the art.

Ballet is essentially an art of tradition, a tradition that is a living force. Music has its score, the drama its book, and the paintings of the past can be seen on the walls of museums and to a certain extent in reproduction. Ballet enjoys no such advantages. The tradition is handed down from master to master. Cease dancing for twenty years and the damage might well be beyond repair. When the great dancer dies, nothing but a name and sometimes a legend would seem to remain. That is the superficial view. Tradition has been enriched by every great dancer, and something of her contribution to the art survives and is taught in the classrooms and on the stage. Taglioni, Zucchi, Pavlova have left behind them a very positive contribution to the art they graced, though it might be difficult to analyse it in words. For this reason I have started the book with a brief historical sketch. The average theatre-goer may have seen or read a Greek tragedy; he will almost certainly have seen a play by Shakespeare. The theatrical producer, the young Academy student, and the dramatic critic will all be familiar with the drama of the past. It is rightly considered an indispensable part of theatrical education. But no dancing school teaches the history of ballet, few dancing teachers themselves know the origin of the steps they are teaching or their æsthetic significance. Yet such knowledge is both practical and indispensable. Physically the young dance pupil is better trained than her actress sister, she works harder, she has more technical virtuosity. But mentally there can be no comparison. The actress from a reputable school is taught to think, the dancer to perform steps that are meaningless in themselves. "*Dance with your head,*" said Pavlova; the thousands of young dancers who graduate annually can only dance with their feet. The trade of dancing flourishes, but the art suffers. And it is important today that the art of dancing should flourish in this country.

Dancing knows no language barriers, consequently ballet is the greatest shop-window for a nation's art. Russia realised this (she still does. Was not *Swan Lake* chosen for the edification of Anthony Eden and other distinguished visiting diplomats?), and what we know of Russia artistically first came to us' through the Russian Ballet. We saw and applauded Karsavina; she showed us the art of Alexandre Benois, Leon Bakst, Nathalie Gontcharova, and others; through her we first heard the music of Stravinsky. The realisation that Russia was not at that time a far-removed and semi-barbarous country may have turned many to Russian literature and drama. There is nothing far-fetched in the supposition. On the Continent today England is thought of as being backward in music and painting. She is known mainly through her football, her bad cooking, and the excellent cut of her suits, important but limited, and sometimes even the football matches are lost. The ballet, better than a hundred concerts or exhibitions of painting opened by epigrammatic ambassadors, can convince people to the contrary. They will be learning without conscious effort. I have purposely stressed this utilitarian angle of ballet, since art for art's sake is not at this time such a popular slogan as art for propaganda's sake, and ballet is legitimate propaganda and not *bourrage de crâne* or goebbeling. Today, in order to survive without subsidies, ballet must be popular. Its appeal is no longer restricted to the courtier, the specialist, or the snob.

After sketching the history of ballet from a practical rather than an academic angle, I will deal with the æsthetics of ballet, again from the practical angle of the dancer and her public. In a further section, I will amplify that study by analysing certain " key " ballets that are constantly in the repertoire, attempting nothing so rash as a guide to beauty, but filling in a background that may make the beauty more significant.

The story of modern ballet can best be developed by a study of various outstanding personalities, since an art of tradition depends essentially upon personalities and the impression that they make upon their followers, whose task it will be to preserve and extend the legacy. I will touch only lightly upon certain aspects of the contemporary scene. At the present day activity is so great that any detailed critical account of companies and dancers would be out of date within a few weeks. I will, however, include some mention of the leading dancers of today.

The next few years may well decide the entire future of ballet, so that it is more than ever necessary for those who love the art to temper their enthusiasm with a background of knowledge and tradition. Ballet does need saving from its friends, from the person " who knows what he likes and doesn't know why," as well as from the person who " thinks he knows why." A number of major Russian Ballet companies have created innumerable partisans in search of excitement and hangers-on out for their own profit. Dancers and public suffer. The quality of the work alone matters. This cannot be sufficiently stressed. It may be that Russian Ballet is about to be strangled by unscrupulous methods, by ridiculous pygmies who do not know the difference between *Swan Lake* and *Les Sylphides*. The unfortunate artists, treated like stocks and shares, are helpless in their hands. The public, by adopting a critical attitude, can help.[1]

Ballet is an expressive art without language barriers. Such an art is certainly of value just now.

---

[1] Today this is a problem for the American ballet public.

CHAPTER 2

The Historical Background

*The place and nature of ballet—The first important ballet
—The birth of professional ballet—Technique and artistry,
a permanent struggle—Noverre—The influence of Milan
—The Romantic Ballet—The decline of ballet—The
origins of Russian Ballet.*

(I)

THERE are various ways of treating the history of ballet :
technically, socially, or æsthetically. The technical, while
it is of the greatest interest when demonstrated, is dull and
almost meaningless in description. I shall therefore refer
to technical development but indirectly, and concentrate on
the social and æsthetic aspects of ballet history. This
chapter is merely a sketch with many omissions. Its purpose here is to serve as a background for what follows, and
as a hint of the fascination and importance of the subject.

There is one initial conception without which it is impossible to understand ballet : it is the vital conception that
nearly all young ballet dancers ignore. *Ballet is a modern
art, dancing is prehistoric. The history of ballet is but a
fragment of the history of dancing.* It may interest us the
most, but it is far from being the most important. Dancing
belongs to the village, the temple, the church, and, most
recently, the stage. Dancing may be indulged in for the
sheer pleasure of the performer, because the performer is
frightened and wishes to placate an angry god, because it
has become a ceremonial and the performer no longer
knows its exact significance, because the performer wishes
to entertain a public. Dancing may be entirely spontaneous
—David dancing before the Ark; guided by a simple pattern—the Morris dance; or highly complex and only possible to the specialist—ballet.

We are interested in dancing that belongs to the stage,

that has its being because the performer wishes to entertain a public, and that is highly complex in form and only possible to the specialist. Such dancing existed in the heyday of Greek culture, was known to the Roman Emperors and practised by them, journeyed from Italy to France, and was, so to speak, codified by the logical French mind to become the art we know today.

Ballet, in the form that we recognise it, had its being with the founding of *L'Académie Nationale de la Danse* by Louis XIV, in 1661. *We are able to trace its development in an unbroken line of dancers and teachers from then until the present day.*[1]

The germ that was to develop into ballet was brought into France from Italy by Catherine de Medici, who was eager to divert her sons while she busied herself in ruling. The spectacle was a combination of dancing, singing, and recitation. Its aim was social. It constituted an elegant pastime for the monarch and his court, an opportunity for bawdy humour, for lavish expenditure, and for the fulsome flattery of court to King. The subjects chosen were largely mythological; the King played at godship, the court worshipped. Astute minds, bent on politics rather than pleasure, used the fashionable craze for purposes of national propaganda, among other things, to point out to foreign ambassadors the might of France; much as Hitler once performed his goose-step, but more elegant and subtle, as becomes the French. The finest artistic minds of the day contributed to the music, the decoration, and the poetry of the spectacle. The people paid. The first dramatic ballet of importance from which the history of the art may be said to begin was *Le Ballet Comique de la Reyne* in 1581.

It was mounted by Catherine's first valet, Baldassarino Belgiojoso, an Italian who took the French name of Baltasar de Beaujoyeux. He was considered the best violinist of his day, and for a long time afterwards the first violin continued the functions of dancing master. The teacher

[1] For the story of that pedigree, see the author's *Ballet Panorama*.

of dancing with his little kit is familiar in the work of Hogarth; Dickens mentions it at the class of Mr. Turveydrop in *Bleak House*; Prince Turveydrop fiddled while his father revealed deportment. It was only later that there was a sharp division between the musician and the dancer, a fact that it will be well to remember.

This first notable ballet was to celebrate the wedding of Mademoiselle de Vaudemont, the Queen's sister, to one of the King's *mignons,* Le Duc de Joyeuse. It told the story of a hero who escaped from the wiles of Circe through the intervention of the gods: a thinly veiled allegory. The ladies of the court, unaccustomed to dancing, which was almost exclusively a male pursuit, took part in what was the first *corps de ballet*. The steps of the dance being severely limited, de Beaujoyeux showed extraordinary invention in his pattern and production. " Archimedes himself," said Beaujoyeux, " could not have understood geometrical proportions better than the princesses and ladies practised them in this ballet." In planning a sumptuous spectacle to celebrate one happy occasion, he had laid the foundations of a new art form.

Under Louis XIV the dance developed still further. The King himself was an expert dancer who created an extraordinary number and variety of roles between 1651 and 1669, sometimes appearing in the same ballet under a number of different guises, from low comedy to an impersonation of the gods and heroes of antiquity. He enjoyed the collaboration of the greatest men of his day: the field-marshal de Bassompierre, a *premier danseur* between compaigns, so enthusiastic a dancer that he even worded a battle dispatch in terms of ballet, dignified parliamentary councillors and indolent courtiers who, devoting their whole time to the dance, became semi-professionals. Molière conceived subjects for ballets and advised in their production. Each one of his comedies contained dancing scenes, and many ballets introduced comedies. The two were not yet distinct. Lully and Beauchamps were the dancing-master musicians of the court. Already the art was becoming firmly planted in French soil.

There were professional dancers at this time: gipsies, tumblers and acrobats, rogues and vagabonds, wandering from fair to fair amusing the crowds with their capers, far removed from the elegants who danced to amuse themselves and their friends. To this day ballet dancers and circus folk alone in the theatre maintain a tradition of aloofness, living in a world of their own, true to their standards and beliefs. *Ballet as we know it was born when the acrobatics of the professional and the aristocratic grace of the courtier were united.* It was under the ægis of Lully and Beauchamps that the ballet became professional, and the change was marked by the foundation by Louis XIV of *L'Académie Nationale de Musique et de la Danse* in 1661, still flourishing today at the Opéra, Paris. The King himself, becoming corpulent, abandoned the dance eight years later and the court followed suit.

The dance made rapid progress, which students can follow in close detail, thanks to the notation of Feuillet, Thoinot Arbeau, and Rameau.

Now, the history of dance technique is closely bound up with the history of costume. The women's costumes at the court of Louis XIV were long and heavy, concealing both legs and feet. There was no chance for virtuosity. There could be a geometrical pattern, but no vertical movement, no escape from the eternal pavane and minuet. The whole history of early dance development lies in the search for elevation. When a ballet of this period required the illusion of flight it was necessary to have recourse to levers and pulleys; machinery took the place of physical effort.

The first *ballerina* to move upwards and so enrich the dance was La Camargo in 1721, and she caused a scandal at the beginning by shortening her skirt just a few inches. The actual costume can be seen in Lancret's famous painting. She brought in the early form of the *entrechat*. Her great contemporary, Sallé, tried to free the dance still further by wearing Greek draperies in a ballet, *Pygmalion*, performed at Covent Garden, but the innovation did not catch on for two hundred years, until the time of Isadora Duncan. Only fourteen years later a pupil of Sallé was dancing in *Pygmalion* in Paris in a hooped skirt. The struggle between heavy skirts and muscular freedom continued until after the French Revolution, when Maillot, the costumier of the French opera, invented tights, and this hypocrisy meant the effective triumph of muscular freedom. Even the Pope sanctioned the usage of tights in the theatres under his jurisdiction, though they had to be blue so as not to suggest the too dangerous colour of flesh!

At the beginning of the seventeenth century, the five positions, basis of the technique of ballet,[1] known today to every week-old dancer, were used in a modified form, and Italian masters recommended a slightly turned-out position of the feet. For a long time French dancing retained the graceful, flowing, non-virtuoso inspiration of the minuet, while the Italians, given to the more violent tarantella, developed the athletic aspect. Although the two became rapidly blended, to this day the French style accentuates grace, the Italian technique. This history is not merely an isolated account of old happenings, but something that serves to explain the current scene. It is impossible to isolate the historical background from the æsthetic.

There is in every art a struggle between technique and artistry, the means and the end, the story to be told and the grammar and words used in its telling. Camargo had found a new liberty, and for some time this new liberty proved so intoxicating that dancing became more or less confined to the marvels that could be accomplished by the legs and feet, hidden for so many years. Far-seeing critics of the period wrote that dancing had become so little expressive of anything dramatic that puppets and machines might easily replace dancers. The ballets of the time consisted of a series of danced entrances, scarcely connected

[1] See Glossary.

PRE-CAMARGO.

CAMARGO.

ROMANTIC COSTUME.

THE CLASSIC "TUTU."

by any idea; what we today term a *divertissement* [1] to distinguish it from a ballet. The means was so novel and entertaining that the end was totally forgotten, a state of things that will recur constantly in this history. *The history of ballet consists of periods of intense technical discovery and development, and then a pause during which some master-mind codifies these discoveries and shows their true use as an art form.*

(II)

The first of these master-minds, a major influence up to the present moment, was J. G. Noverre.

Born in 1727, Noverre is said to have been the son of an aide-de-camp of Charles XII, and destined for a military career. There is much doubt about the exact biographical details. He early became a pupil of Louis Dupré, and made his début at the age of sixteen. His first great success as a choreographer was *Fêtes Chinoises,* with décors by François Boucher. He was summoned to Drury Lane by David Garrick, and the great actor, who flatteringly called him " the Shakespeare of the dance," undoubtedly had a strong influence on his work and outlook. Owing to the outbreak of hostilities between France and England on the first night of his London season, he was forced to beat a hasty retreat. This misfortune was typical of his whole life. As a man of choleric disposition he found it difficult to settle down, in spite of a success that won him the esteem of Voltaire and others, and for fifty years he wandered all over Europe, spreading his ideas through his example and more especially through his famous *Lettres sur la Danse,* published in 1760, a manifesto on the art of ballet valued for all time.

We can trace the influence, not only of his letters, but of his ballets and of his teaching.

The theme of his letters may be summarised very roughly as follows: dancing like painting must be inspired

[1] See Glossary.

by Nature. The choreographer is like a painter and must follow similar laws of composition. If ballet is degenerate, it is because, like fireworks, it has been content to remain a pleasure for the eyes alone. Steps have become a meaningless formula. This is not the fault of the art itself. *The well-composed ballet should be a living painting of the drama, character, and customs of mankind; it must be acted, as moving in its effect as a declamation, so that it can speak through the eyes to the soul.* The laws of drama apply to ballet, which must have an introduction, a development, and a climax. If one had to summarise the teaching of Noverre in one sentence—I strongly advise all dancers to turn to his letters—that sentence would be : *Ballet is not an excuse for dancing; dancing in ballet is the means of expressing a dramatic idea.*

I will analyse and comment on this teaching at some greater length in the section on the æsthetic of ballet. From the point of view of history it is sufficient to say that ballet as an art flourished when Noverre's precepts were remembered and acted upon and declined when they were forgotten.

Another great *maître de ballet* and theorist, Angiolini, had an acrimonious pamphlet debate with Noverre on the subject of dramatic ballet, and it is worth mentioning one of his points, which is of great practical value. He attacks the long written programme explanations of Noverre's ballets, which are indeed heavy and uninspired, maintaining that a ballet is a self-confessed failure if it requires a programme explanation to make it clear, a point that Fokine has reiterated throughout his career.

As an active worker Noverre's influence was the greatest at Stuttgart, where he remained for eight years in charge of a company of a hundred *corps de ballet* and twenty principals, placed at his disposal by the art-loving Duke of Württemberg, Charles Eugene. " You are a Prometheus," Voltaire told him; " you must form men and breathe life into them." Stuttgart became a centre of ballet activity, and the greatest dancers of the day flocked there to appear in Noverre's productions, among them the great Vestris, Heinel, Dauberval, and Gardel.

Each one of these dancers has played an important role in the development of ballet which it is not necessary to trace here. Mademoiselle Heinel invented and launched the *pirouette*,[1] which Gardel and Vestris perfected, and they in their turn developed the *rond de jambes*.[1] Today, ballet would be inconceivable without these movements in its repertoire. One of Noverre's most slashing attacks, implicit in his wish to develop pantomime, was made on the mask, which it was customary for dancers to wear. This was abolished almost accidentally by Gardel, who, substituting at the last moment for Vestris, made it a condition that he should appear without a mask and did so with striking success.

(III)

The most notable *ballerina* of this period, famous right up to the French Revolution and after, was Madeleine Guimard, "La Guimard," who fulfilled all that Noverre expected of a dancer, subordinating technique to dramatic expression. The French Revolution brought a temporary halt to the development of ballet in France, though under the Terror the social dance flourished. The centre of interest became focused in Italy once again, where two brilliant men turned thoughts towards ballet and away from opera.

The first, Salvatore Vigano, 1769–1821, a nephew of the composer Boccherini and through his master Dauberval in contact with Noverre's ideals, was a man of wide knowledge, who composed the music for his own ballets, which have been highly praised by Stendhal; too highly, he ranked them higher than Shakespeare. He greatly developed the use of the *corps de ballet* in the modern sense of the word, as an *ensemble* of individuals and not merely

[1] See Glossary.

24

as a symmetrical background. Noverre had constantly railed against the deadly symmetry of the *corps de ballet*. Vigano's works and the trouble in France brought the leading French dancers to Milan, preparing the way for the second great *maître de ballet*. Carlo Blasis, 1803, a pupil of Gardel and Dauberval, is with Noverre the biggest figure in the development of ballet. In his *Treatise on the Art of Dancing,* he summed up and codified what was known, and his system is, in its broad principles, the one in use today. He is the father of classical ballet technique. He paid tribute to Noverre's æsthetic, remarking that only the technical portions were out of date. He was a keen student of sculpture and anatomy, and so lucid a writer that he was able to make clear for all time the mechanical basis of ballet technique. His best-known "invention" is the *attitude*,[1] derived from Gian Bologna's Mercury. Both Noverre and Blasis stress the importance of a knowledge of painting and sculpture for the dancer. Their modern counterparts today, Fokine and Massine, are essentially museum men, as their compositions reveal, but museum men with an understanding, as Noverre insists, of the life that goes on around them. Blasis was a universal genius, a writer, and student of every type of art as well as of politics. His influence on the ballet is a powerful proof that it is not sufficient for the dancer just to dance.

As valuable as his writings was the foundation of the great Academy of Dancing at Milan in 1837, a hundred and seventy-six years after the foundation of the French Academy. His rules have become a model that every institution has tried to follow. Pupils were not admitted before the age of eight or after the age of twelve; fourteen in the case of boys. They had to be medically sound and of good stock. Their training was fully mapped out: three hours' practice a day and one hour of mime. They were attached to the school for eight years, and after that their future was assured by an ascending scale of salaries.

[1] See Glossary.

This should do away with the superstition that it is necessary to start ballet training at the age of five, six, or even earlier—a superstition that must have caused, and is still causing, untold damage. A parent who takes her baby to ballet class is an idiot; the teacher who receives her something very much worse. The baby can learn dancing, but only eurhythmics or something of a pre-ballet type that is both healthy and of musical value. Apart from the physical damage, the mental effect of rigid ballet discipline at an early age is deplorable, killing originality, spontaneity, and the essential joy of dancing. The great Russian *ballerinas,* who have set the standards for future generations, started without exception at the age of ten. This is but one of the practical lessons of ballet history.

Every boy and girl today who perform their arduous exercises at the *barre* [1] and in the centre are paying an unconscious tribute to the science of the great master, Carlo Blasis. Many of the teachers today, both Russian and English, are closely descended from him, since his pupil Giovanni Lepri taught Enrico Cecchetti, master of the Russian Ballet, and of so many English dancers. The thought is an inspiring one. The smallest pupil should have some conception of the dignity and history of her art.

(IV)

The period that is best known to the layman through the many beautiful coloured lithographs that survive is that of the romantic ballet. These delicately tinted, highly idealised pictures of the great *ballerinas* Taglioni, Cerrito, Elssler, Grisi, Grahn, that decorate the rooms of so many of the dancers of today, have a great deal to tell us if we study them with care. No photographs could be so revealing. Cerrito floats over a waterfall, Taglioni walks among the tree-tops to gather a nest, moves across a meadow without disturbing a blade of grass. There are wings to suggest movement, never muscles. These charm-

[1] See Glossary.

ing drawings tell of an age of extreme artificiality, where the dance is used to exploit a new æsthetic, a period of great dancers idolised by their public, who forgot the art of ballet in their enthusiasm for the individual. The romantic ballet began in a blaze of glory, and in a comparatively short time burnt itself out, until only in Russia a serious public for ballet remained.

Noverre had postulated a close contact with Nature; romanticism denied it. The main influence of the romantic period was not a dancer at all but a poet, Théophile Gautier, a fact that has a very important bearing on the development of the ballet.

The romantic ballet was one aspect of a whole movement that swept over France and the rest of Europe, beginning in 1830. Its idols were Heine and Walter Scott, its greatest products the drama of Victor Hugo, the painting of Delacroix, and the music of Berlioz. " Banish reality," said the romantics; " art must be an escape into an enchanted realm." Revolution was conceived romantically, as in Delacroix' great painting, " Sur les Barricades "; only later was it to be viewed solely as a problem in economics, persecution, protective custody, and mass murder. The ballet, ever a sensitive instrument in the hands of artists, the ballet that created a world of illusion, however realistically it was handled, was ideal for the spread of romantic conceptions. The fairy, the wili, the witch, and the vampire swept away the heroes of antiquity, the pale German moonlight of Goethe replaced Olympus. Man was no longer the hero, gone the days of a Vestris; woman was idealised, and man must be content to remain in the background and lift her when necessary—a conception that upset the whole orchestration of dancing.

In the early seventeenth century ballet was exclusively a male art, in the early eighteenth century man was on sufferance. The romantics could not interfere too strenuously in the technique of dancing, but, since the dancer was almost an immortal, the technique did not greatly interest

Gautier, and at times he spoke slightingly of it, though as a critic he was too great to admit indifferent work. The one great technical development of the period was the use of the tips of the toes—*les pointes*—the ideal taking-off position for flight. Ever since the discovery of the points they have been abused, and, more than anything, have brought the art of ballet into disrepute with thinking people. I shall have a great deal to say about this when I come to analyse technique.

The central figure of the period is a non-dancer, Théophile Gautier, but the *maître de ballet* who translated its ideals was Philippe Taglioni, important both as choreographer and father and teacher of the great Marie Taglioni. None of his ballets has survived. From all accounts his early ones were of considerable interest, while his later work degenerated into a formula that finally killed romanticism.

Marie Taglioni was a great dancer, unusual in her extraordinary frailty, that gave her an ethereal appearance. She is considered the leader of romanticism; her ballet *La Sylphide* stood for a manifesto of the movement, yet from all accounts she was more purely classical than romantic, which presupposes a certain flamboyance that her rival Elssler possessed. Taglioni has been called "the first Christian dancer," so free from sex appeal was her art, and slightly hostile critics even reproached her with being a dancer for women.

The fierce rivalry between Taglioni and Elssler did much to popularise ballet by fanning the spirit of partisanship that is known in every gallery queue today—and in the stalls. Of all the great dancers of that period the one closest to us is surely Carlotta Grisi, creator of the role of *Giselle,* a ballet that is in the permanent repertoire both of our own Sadler's Wells and the Opéra, Paris. It has survived close on a hundred years, the only romantic ballet to reach us intact. *La Sylphide* belongs to legend—its name is very charmingly suggested in a new romantic

28

ballet that has rid itself of the conventional trappings and retained the spirit—but *Giselle* is fact. It links Grisi, Pavlova, Karsavina, Spessivtseva,[1] and our own Margot Fonteyn; Paris, St. Petersburg, and London. If from our experience we talk of romantic ballet, it is *Giselle* we mean. I will analyse it at some length as a type of ballet, but this is the context from which it comes.

With the decline of the great dancers of the period, the popularity of ballet rapidly waned, for without these great dancers what remained? The principles of Noverre were utterly forgotten, ballet was no longer an art but a spectacle for the eye of the tired business man, and the Edwardian business man could be tired, although the phrase did not yet exist. The ballet no longer interested serious musicians. The turning out of ballet music had become an industry. In every branch of art, romanticism was being brushed aside by realism, in its turn to be ousted by impressionism. The ballet had been one of the means of expression of a movement no longer in vogue. The male dancer scarcely existed; just row upon row of pretty, grinning, well-corseted girls, a *foyer de la danse* where the elegants could meet and flirt with them in the intervals, and a number of " rats "—as the members of the Paris Opéra *corps de ballet* were called—whose greatest justification was to serve as models for the master Degas.

Two hundred years after the founding of the Academy, ballet in the country of its birth was artistically bankrupt. The art that had been raised by a powerful dynasty of kings, nourished by the genius of a Boucher, Boquet, Lully, Molière, dignified by the interest of a Voltaire, that had produced men of the mental attainments of a Noverre, had become merely a prelude to flirtation, the dancers *grisettes* and expert gold-diggers. It is well for us to remember that this occurred but a decade or two after one of the greatest booms in its history, when the attitude of the audience was very close to what it is today.

[1] In Western Europe abbreviated to Spessiva.

The same was the case in England. The popularity of the romantic ballet had spread from Paris. London was noted for the warmth of its audiences. Théophile Gautier viewed them with a certain amount of suspicion. He was not willing to accept a London reputation without a severe test. There were English dancers, but these were minor figures, the most famous being Adelina Plunkett and the ill-fated Clara Webster, burned to death when her dress caught fire on the stage at Drury Lane. In England, without a State institution to maintain at any rate the technical tradition, the fate of ballet was still worse. It became a popular feature of the music-hall programme, packing the Empire and the Alhambra. Many of the dancers were excellent, among them Adeline Genée, Lydia Kyasht, and our own Phyllis Bedells; but the ballets themselves would scarcely have won the approval of Noverre. They were the exact type of thing from which Fokine was revolting, but without the academic purity that was some justification. The ballet was rescued from this lamentable fall by the Russians, who invaded Paris in 1909 and London two years later, to remain in occupation ever since.

(v)

The history of ballet in Russia belongs to the past, and is in its right place here; the history of Russian Ballet belongs to the present, and probably, if the present-day Russians will learn the meaning of the word *collaboration*, to the future.

There is a mention of Russian dancers at the court of Louis XIV, when some " Muscovites " came to learn the art and gravely displeased their teachers by their lack of attention. Dancing, however, received its first great impetus at the time of Peter the Great, 1672–1725. It was a part of his general policy to Westernise Russia, bound up with his costume reforms and with his forcing of the boyars to shave their beards. We have already seen the intimate link between costume and dance. This is but one more vivid proof. Dancing is the most positive and striking expression of the national characteristics of a people. Change their dances and you may change their mentality. In Russia the women were kept apart from the men. Introduce social dances, routs, and assemblies, make them compulsory, and Eastern seclusion must give way to Westernisation. Peter the Great realised this just as Kemal Ataturk has today. Shave the men's beards, remove their dignified and cumbersome robes, and they became eligible partners for the dance. It may be necessary to imprison a few, to antagonise the Church. No matter. Peter was a dictator, and one of his aims was to impose upon a backward people the social dance of the West. The theatrical art of ballet has grown out of the social dance; the steps, originally performed for pleasure, are the basis of the classical ballet. In Russia ballet followed the same evolution, more rapidly because there were examples from abroad. Peter forced the art of his country into a new channel, just as he forced the armament by land and sea. Where the dictators in Italy and Germany have thought nationally, Peter, in every way a more enlightened man, had vision enough to think internationally and to borrow what was best from abroad, until he had planted it firmly in his country: painting, architecture, fashions, the army and navy. By so doing, he permanently enriched his country instead of impoverishing it in the present-day fashion. . . . *Alas, poor Salzburg!*

In the succeeding reigns under foreign guidance the art of ballet began to be planted in a country now conscious of the meaning of dancing. The Empress Anne (1693–1740) founded the Academy, which survives today under a different régime, importing a Frenchman, Landé, to direct it, and thinking it of sufficient importance to include dancing in the curriculum of the cadets. The Empress Elizabeth, a great beauty, was herself fond of dancing, and brought over an Austrian *maître de ballet,* Hilferding, with many of the latest works.

It was with Catherine the Great (1762–1796) that the most intense development took place. Le Picq, a Frenchman, and the great Italian Angiolini came to her court and spread both knowledge and enthusiasm.

Ballet might well have remained a popular and " borrowed " art, as it had done in England, but for one factor that distinguishes the history of Russian Ballet.

England enjoyed the art. The greatest dancers from abroad visited London and filled their pockets. Yet there was never a trace of a native English ballet until the present day. England remained " good audience " throughout. Russia began to dance. This may be partly due to historical reasons. During the reigns of Henry VIII and Elizabeth the court enjoyed elaborate masks, but the growth of Protestantism in its puritanical form meant the decay of Merrie England, and one of the most musical of nations became a consumer instead of a creator.

In Russia the court set the example and the people followed. The geography of Russia is responsible. The nobles possessed vast estates and quantities of serfs at their command, slaves of the same creed and race, who were not given their freedom until 1861. So large and remote were these estates that it was necessary for the nobles to provide their own comforts and amusements. The Empress favoured ballet, her courtiers followed suit. They trained their serfs and formed ballet troupes of their own. The whole Russian theatre owes its origin to the serf actors. This meant that ballet became a part of the people, not merely an entertainment provided from without. In Russia, ballet had a greater contact with humanity than in any other country. It could not be destroyed, as it had been in France, by any wave of artificiality; it could not become the very passive instrument of a group of poets. The peasant is by nature a realist, and Russian Ballet, even in its most romantic phases, has always retained, comparatively speaking, a close touch with reality.

Bit by bit these private troupes became merged in the

central organisations of St. Petersburg and Moscow, the dancers so selected gaining their freedom before the general emancipation of the serfs. The ballet school started as a system of patronage, but ended with rules as strict as those laid down by Carlo Blasis for Milan. The ballet became the most cherished possession of the Emperor, who lavished immense sums upon its maintenance.

From the time of Catherine onwards, the history of Russian Ballet consists of the gradual absorption of foreign knowledge by the Russians themselves until the art is indigenous and Russian Ballet alone exists as an active creative artistic force, producing its own Noverre, its own Blasis, its own Lully, its own Boquet. The succession of foreign visitors: Didelot, who had the greatest scholastic influence; Dupré, and Taglioni, who had the most enthusiastic triumph of her career, left not merely pleasant memories but a tradition that was assimilated. Russian dancers began to make a reputation, among them Andreyanova, who danced *Giselle* very shortly after its creation, the tragic Danilova and Istomina, sung by Russian poets.

Soon the stage is dominated by Russian *ballerinas,* Sokolova and Vasem being outstanding, though the guidance is in the hands of three foreigners, two of whom became completely Russianised.

Ballet in Russia became Russian Ballet through Marius Petipa, a Frenchman, Gustave Johannsen, a Dane, and Enrico Cecchetti, an Italian. The account of their influence belongs rightly to the modern scene, but before developing the story of modern ballet and introducing the major figures in contemporary ballet, it will be necessary to analyse the art itself and to postulate certain standards. Only in this way can we appreciate what is happening at the present moment.

CHAPTER 3

The Æsthetic Background

*Criticism—A definition of ballet—The dancers; their attri-
butes—Technique—The border-line between acrobatics and
dancing—Types of dancer—The choreographer; definition
of choreography; his attributes; nature of his art—Music
and its possible relations to movement—The décor and its
function—The literary element; theme and narrative—
Æsthetics and economics—The making of a dancer: in
practice—Outlets for the dancer: ballet clubs, examinations, and competitions.*

THE criticism of the ballet was highly developed during
the formative period, both by dancers and encyclopædists.
Up till the time of Théophile Gautier, it continued as a
serious subject for study. Gautier's impressions of dancers
are so vivid that we can discuss Taglioni, Elssler, Grisi,
and Grahn almost as if we had seen them. Ballet came to
be considered as too frivolous for serious attention only
during the decay of romanticism, when it left the opera
house for the music hall. The naughty 'nineties and the
traditional draught of champagne in the dancer's slipper
are difficult memories to live down, obliterating the memory
of such *balletomanes* as Voltaire and Stendhal. In Russia,
where ballet never sank so low, there were many remarkable writers on the subject, starting with Volinsky, who
learnt to dance at the age of seventy, Plestchaeff, Svetloff,
and André Levinson. They not only interpreted the finer
points of the art to the public, but acted as mentors to the
dancers themselves. Their criticism was both respected
and feared.

In Western Europe, since the advent of Diaghileff,
ballet almost took its place once again as a serious and
respectable subject; the champagne-filled slipper was given
a rest. However, in England and France ballet criticism

became the exclusive property of the music critic, and music is but one part of ballet. The dramatic critic, the art critic, or a critic of dancing might consider that they had equal claims. Though of them all the music critic is probably the closest to ballet, as a specialist he may well be biased; and while he influences public opinion, his other important function of influencing the dancers themselves is gone.

This difficulty of finding the appropriate critic will show us as a start the complex nature of our study. The would-be critic is still further handicapped by the fact that he has no score or printed word to which he can refer. He must rely upon eyes and memory, pass a judgment on music, choreography, dancing, décors and costumes, drama, and the combined effect of all these things together, for ballet is a combination of these elements. When he has noticed all these things he has a good half-hour in which to condense his opinions into two hundred and fifty words.

To understand ballet we must analyse each separate element, and we meet with an initial difficulty: that of where to begin. They are by no means in watertight compartments. It will be necessary for the critic to affix little labels here and there purely for the sake of convenience. Ballet is a particularly difficult subject about which to write, since it is quite impossible to make quotations.

It seems safest to start with a definition. I suggest the following: *Ballet is a form of theatrical entertainment that tells a story, develops a theme, or suggests an atmosphere through the orchestration of a group of costumed dancers trained according to strict rules and guided in tempo and spirit by the music, against a decorative background; music, movement, and decoration being parallel in thought.*

What a cumbersome formula for anything so simply and obviously beautiful as *Les Sylphides,* or for anything so deeply and obviously moving as *Petrouchka*! Yet an examination of this kind can bring out fresh beauties in each work by insisting on a certain standard of performance.

Let us start with the dancers, those partners in the composite whole that is ballet who are nearest to the audience, who interpret the music, the idea, and the choreography, and who wear the costumes.

(A) THE DANCERS

Dancers vary enormously in physique, type, and temperament, but there are certain attributes that all require.

The first essential is a suitable physique. I hesitate for the moment to use the word beauty, though it is an obvious advantage, because beauty is altogether too vague a word. The modern sex appeal, too, is not accurate. One cannot and should not rule out sex from ballet, but the difference between ballet and some other forms of dancing is that they deliberately exploit sex while ballet does not, unless the theme of the work calls for it. Some superficial, smart-aleck or disordered minds have seen in the present-day craze for ballet nothing but sex, an altogether too easy judgment. For some types of mind the sex appeal of the dancers may be an inducement to visit the ballet, but they will find it in a far more practical and concentrated form in cabaret and non-stop variety, and are scarcely likely to become *balletomanes* on that score. The dancer requires the type of charm that a fair number of her audience will call beauty, and for a very obvious reason. Her face and her body are the instrument upon which she plays. While a violinist may possess both genius and technique, no one will be aware of the fact if his fiddle is poor in quality. He will spend thousands upon a Stradivarius or an Amati; the dancer must be born with the perfect instrument and develop it by training.

We have seen from our historical background that it is wrong to consider dancing purely from the point of view of the movements of the legs. The dancer must be completely expressive from head to foot. *The face is as much a part of the dancer's instrument as the feet and arms.* Many a dexterous performer is of no artistic significance through

36

an adenoidal expression and a hanging jaw. Oh, those Sylphides with their permanent air of acute bellyache, mixture of boredom and stupidity! Many a technical shortcoming has been compensated for by an expressive face that holds the attention. There are many hundreds today in the dancing schools who are doomed to disappointment because they have not had the good fortune to be built as dancers.

Under the heading of physical aptitude, I would include natural grace. The highly developed technical ballet dancer is by no means necessarily graceful. The highly trained dancer's manner of walking is often flippantly known as " the *ballerina* waddle," a penguin-like method of locomotion. Technique can always be acquired, grace and ease of movement but rarely. Faulty teaching may ruin natural grace. *One of the aims of teaching is not merely to add something to the pupil, but to take advantage of what is there already.* Had quantity and not quality been the aim, Pavlova might never have had the opportunity of enchanting us with her art. Hers was a particular case, and every worthwhile dancer is a particular case, with an individual physique that must be studied and especially fitted into the classical framework. There is no infallible system, there are fortunately a few inspired teachers.

The next point to be considered is the pupil's musicality. It is obvious that she must possess an ear for rhythm. That is unfortunately the exclusive sense in which the musicality of dancers is usually considered. It is the bare minimum requirement without which the dancer is not fitted to appear at all. Its higher sense, the one which distinguishes the *corps de ballet* dancer from the *ballerina,* lies in a far more subtle understanding and appreciation of musical content and atmosphere. *The music speaks to the dancer, the dancer interprets the music to the audience.* This will become clearer if I lay down a parallel with the legitimate stage. There the actress interprets the plot and idea of an author with words chosen by that author. The dancer interprets a choreographer's idea with movements devised by the choreographer, but an idea that never comes to life unless she receives guidance from the music. Let us take the extreme case of a completely plotless ballet, *Les Sylphides,* which contains the essence of romanticism with none of its hobgoblin trappings. There is nothing to guide the dancer here save the music. She is performing certain rhythmic movements, but that is not enough. She must convey to her audience a particular atmosphere. For that reason only the truly musical dancer can succeed in interpreting *Les Sylphides,* one of the most frequently performed yet most rarely interpreted of all ballets. It is when ballet is understood in the Noverre-Fokine sense of the word that the dancer needs true musicality. During the degeneracy of ballet, when music is merely an accompaniment, the dancer requires but a good ear and a dramatic sense that is something apart. In the musical ballet, as distinct from the ballet with music, the ability to act and the ability to understand music are very closely linked together. The next point to be considered, therefore, is the ability to mime.

We have seen the importance assigned to this in our historical survey and the early distinction between the merely technical performer and the truly interpretative artist. Miming in dancing sets a difficult problem. It is, as we have seen, often closely associated with a musical sense; it is also rigidly controlled by the movements assigned to the dancer. Mime in ballet varies from the purely conventional sign language of the romantic period ballet (hand on heart means love) to the skilled acting of the Fokine dance dramas. It must never be thought of as something superimposed on to the movements of the dance, but as a part of the dancing itself. Miming that forces itself on the attention is bad, usually showing that the face is making a violent effort to compensate for the shortcomings of the body. When I come to deal with type ballets I will consider the isolated and exceptionally important case of *Giselle*. While this calls for very definite interpretation, every role in ballet requires mime, even when the *ballerina* is most herself in some sparkling virtuoso variation.

The other attributes required by the dancer before we come to discuss the problem of technique are simpler to imagine, more difficult to describe on paper.

Personality is a common attribute required in every artistic pursuit. In dancing it means style, movement that is controlled by the mind, instead of being a physical reaction prompted by classroom habit. Once again we are led back to music. *Personality in dancing, among other things, implies an individual reaction to the meaning of the music as against the muscular reaction inspired by the rhythm of the music.* It is astonishing to what a degree the dancer can become a puppet devoid of all personality, and yet earn tremendous applause from a public that can count up to fifty.

I distrust profoundly all superficial use of that much-abused word "temperament," usually employed by the English public in its sexual significance, to point out the artistic shortcomings of the English girl. There is nothing more deceitful than an assumed temperament that consists in making oneself seen and heard at all costs by a number of deliberate and unworthy tricks. It has proved the undoing of more than one dancer, who deceives a certain number of people part of the time. The Spanish dance is the one usually martyred by dancers who think a great deal about temperament: usually the English girl with an inferiority complex. *Temperament* in dancing, if it implies anything that can be analysed, *means natural vivacity and self-confidence, something that is felt with such sincere conviction that it becomes a burning necessity to convey it across the footlights.* In that sense it is an indispensable attribute that cannot be learnt. Let us be original and omit its customary sexual implications. Girls of all nations have lovers.

Intelligence is another attribute that the dancer of today more than ever requires. In the past the dancer received a true education as distinct from physical training. Music, painting, and the meaning of her art were analysed for her by experienced teachers. She faced her audience with some knowledge of what she was doing, a positive consciousness of the structure of which she formed a part. The present-day dancer, for reasons chiefly economic, is trained purely acrobatically. If she is to survive as an artist, it becomes vital for her to form a background of her own. The Maryinsky *ballerina* can discuss ballet; the average young dancer of today, steps. (A love of gossip is common to both, and to critics as well.) Lack of intelligence plus a lack of education condemns the dancer after a burst of precocity to complete artistic sterility.

I have purposely left all consideration of technique to the end. It is a complex subject that will need a quantity of convenient labels. *Technique is a means and never an end.* Most ballet dancers, and through them all the opponents of ballet, never realise that fact. It is vital and should be printed on a placard in every schoolroom in the kingdom and solemnly intoned before the class. The numerous exams that are the goal of most teachers and pupils in England completely obscure that fact, making technique the end. Perhaps the exams are not to blame; there is much to be said for them, but their application and the attitude of the teachers is usually indefensible. Technique is sufficient when it enables the dancer to express with fluency both herself and the role she is undertaking. If she or her public worry about the technique, it is clearly insufficient. *Technique does not mean the performance, however perfect, of isolated steps.* The artist-dancer does not think in terms of steps, but conceives the dance as a whole, melting one step into the next. The dancer who reveals the join between the steps, the staccato dancer—and ninety per cent are—is as bad as the actor who stammers. Unfortunately, the public usually mistakes the staccato dancer, who underlines her difficulties, for the brilliant dancer. Applause is only too often a sign of the consciousness that something difficult has just been attempted. The truly moving passage is received with the rare compliment of silence before the final burst of applause. Unrestrained and unreasoning applause have been extremely damaging, especially in the beginning at Sadler's Wells, where the dancers were making a strong effort to sort out their knowledge of the art. There, applause revealed a strong tendency to become merely partisan. Sporting, perhaps, but unsound. The audience is showing marked improvement of late.

It is necessary here to pause and consider the difference between virtuoso dancing and acrobatics. Opponents of ballet as a system, such as Isadora Duncan, can see no difference, and often in practice there is no difference. *The difference between dancing and acrobatics lies not so much in technique as in a state of mind.*

It is possible for the same movements to be performed to the same music by two different individuals and in one case to be pure dancing, in the other case acrobatics.

The pure dancer performs his steps, however complex, with the conception of the dance as a whole, being guided by the music, concealing his difficulties, and making his climax an artistic one. He is depicting a definite idea.

The acrobat performs his steps in such a fashion as to underline the difficulty of the task. In his case the drama is implicit in the physical performance. He is putting a question to the audience: " Will I get through without a tumble or not? " He is telling them: " Look, I am creating a record number of turns. Will I reach fifty? " That is the only idea behind his performance. His climax consists of a dazzling finish to whip up applause. There is relief in this climax that he has succeeded in overcoming his difficulties. It is like the singer of patriotic or Mother ballads who at the conclusion lifts his hat and waits.

In the first case the audience murmurs: " How beautiful "; in the second case: " How clever."

We shall see that in certain cases, especially in bad periods, the choreographer places an enormous onus on the dancer to steer clear of acrobatics, using difficulties just because they are difficult.

This consideration of technique is important just because the average ballet dancer is incompetent to defend ballet, either through words or dancing, against ill-informed attacks. The playing of the piano is well enough understood as an art for no one to utter such an absurd statement as: " These eternal finger exercises are unnatural and dangerous to all self-expression. Let us throw overboard this elaborate technique and find something natural and simple." Obviously absurd, but then virtuoso pianists have never been considered as particularly frivolous (no one has ever drunk out of their slippers), and, in spite of the popularity of ballet, dancers are still very much misunderstood and not accorded the status they deserve. The system of classical ballet is merely a physical training. There is nothing particularly beautiful in standing on one toe or in turning on that toe a given number of times. There is nothing particularly beautiful about a five-finger exercise. Beauty only comes later in the use to which these things are put. Neither is unnatural in the sense that both can be acquired with ease by the average person; both are unnatural in the sense that all art is unnatural and must be acquired through practice. It is through a misconception of technique that natural movement is always invoked in opposition to ballet. There is only one reply to this: ballet training is comprehensive, other dance training limited. The ballet dancer can perform every type of work: Spanish in *Le Chapeau Tricorne*, Russian in *Prince Igor*, Oriental in *Scheherazade*, Greek in *Daphnis and Chloe*; note that in not one of these ballets is the tip of the toe used at all.

The reason why the independent dancer of the Wigman type can make such a good argument on paper is a superior and bolder intelligence and education. In her devotion to a system the average ballet dancer has ceased to think at all, possessing neither taste nor discrimination. The Duncan or the Wigman, in elaborating a personal system, is compelled to study music, costume, and the meaning of movement. I do not for a moment claim that the great dancer must come out of the classical system. But what I do say is that the great independent dancer would be greater still if she had absorbed the classical system. There has always been a singular monotony in the work that has grown out of so-called natural methods; also in most cases the results have been so very personal that there remained nothing to transmit to pupils. The Pavlova of the *Bacchanal* met Duncan on her own ground, but she was also the Pavlova of *La Péri*, the *Dying Swan*, and that delicious nothing, *Noël*. Had Duncan possessed the fortifying discipline of technique, she would never have presented the pathetic and terrifying picture of her last days. She would either have been in a fit state to continue, or by measuring herself against a known quantity, she would have realised the ruin she had become.

Technique is a known quantity by which the dancer can measure herself. A personally evolved technique, however complex, cannot serve that all-important function.

Dancing that gets its inspiration from ancient Greece is also popular today, and doubtless it is of distinct benefit as physical education. So is hockey. (Both have a thickening effect on the ankles.) Its artistic pedigree will not bear close examination. The dance rests on music. There is no one today who can tell us much about Greek music. To perform movements lifted from a Greek vase to the music of Chopin or Brahms is clearly not performing a Greek dance. The ballet has used on occasions the inspiration of Greek movement, but there is insufficient there to establish a whole technique, and the ballet technique has served its purpose admirably. It is necessary to have a very profound knowledge both of dancing and of choreography to knit the static movements on pottery and bas-relief into a connected whole. It is not sufficient to be photographed in draperies, draped round the Parthenon. Ballet technique may have its faults, but it does provide a tested and extended knowledge of the possibilities of the human body. It is necessary to state once again that a knowledge of that technique in practice must not be the exclusive aim of teachers and their pupils. The dancing rebels do provide one fine ingredient—thought. There is a close parallel here with the unlicensed medical practitioner.

It is not generally realised by the layman that just as there are types of singer—soprano, mezzo-soprano, and contralto—there are types of dancer. The dancer belongs to one type or another by reason both of her physique and, to a lesser degree, of her personality. Physique and personality are closely connected. In our everyday life the beauty is usually sure of herself.

The much-abused term " *ballerina* " has a very positive meaning. In State institutions it is a definite rank in the hierarchy of ballet, just as " general " is a rank that cannot be assumed at will; artistically and in practice, it means the dancer who assumes the leading role in classical ballets. The classical ballet will need elaborating in its proper place. I mentioned the difficulty at the beginning of this section of knowing exactly where to begin.

I can best define the classical dancer by discussing interpretation. All ballet training is classical, depending on the system codified by Carlo Blasis. That system is used for a variety of different ends: to express a positive role; to indicate an atmosphere; to interpret the national dance of some particular country. In the classical ballet the role is subordinated to the technique. Therefore, *the classical dancer holds us by her line and fluency and not by her interpretation of anything positive.* As we have seen, classicism and acrobatics could be considered as very nearly related. I have defined the essential differences. In classical ballet an enormous responsibility rests upon the dancer. She cannot hide behind her role. The music indicates the tempo, the choreographer the movement, the dancer is free, within limits which must be carefully appreciated, to express herself. It is she who must give meaning to what she is doing, since the story is told only every now and then by conventional gesture. The pleasure in watching classical ballet lies in the beauty of line and in the revelation of personality. One dancer may make her *adagio* exciting, another dramatic, a third ethereal, a fourth more tender, and so on. It is only in a classical role that the dancer can be dissected both as a technician and as a personality. Even the costume of classical ballet, the rim of a hoop, the *tutu*,[1] as it is called, is mercilessly revealing, nearly always unbecoming, and wisely abolished by Fokine. No frills, no bluff, no hiding of physical, technical, or artistic imperfections. Classicism, because it is all-revealing, is the point of departure for dancers and audience. It is obvious that the requirements involved are so great that the true *ballerina* is a rarity. Just because her body is her instrument and it is impossible to acquire one save by birth, the *ballerina* is rarer than the concert pianist or the violinist. There are no more than a half-dozen of front rank in a generation.

The good classical *ballerina,* unless she is limited in her mind to the interpretation of purely classical roles, has the necessary equipment to dance nearly every type of role. She is all-inclusive.

The next division, by far the largest and most common, is that of a *demi-caractère*. Here, the technique required is identical, its use is different. The *demi-caractère* dancer interprets a more definite role. As a *ballerina* her role invariably has a name; usually she is a Princess; but that role does not require much interpretation, the dancing alone is the focal point. In *demi-caractère* it is the role itself. The dancer is a Colum-

[1] See illustration, page 21.

bine (*Carnaval*), a soubrette (*Good-humoured Ladies*), and the interpretation of the role is essential to the story. The dancer can conceal herself behind a story and a costume. The choreographer assumes a greater responsibility, he is partly a dramatist. Since there are a variety of different roles and costumes, both mercifully concealing, the dancer does not require the perfect dignity and physique of the *ballerina*.

The third category is that of the character dancer who performs either the heavily mimed roles, the villains and comics of classical ballet, the grotesques (Baba Yaga in *Contes Russes*) or the national dances (*Prince Igor, The Three-cornered Hat*) of a particular country. England, having no national dances, is sadly lacking in character dancers of this type, though English dancers excel in the heavy mime of grotesque ballet (*The Rake's Progress*). The attributes I have outlined apply in a varying degree to each one of these categories. Karsavina excelled in all three—*The Swan* Princess, the Columbine, and the Miller's Wife. The outstanding young *ballerinas* of today, Irina Baronova and Margot Fonteyn, are also catholic in their capabilities.

At the present day the tendency is for all dancers to be *demi-caractère*. The classical ballet is a survival, unfamiliar to the average teacher, and the secret of forming the true *ballerina* belongs to but a few institutions and those teachers who have themselves been *ballerinas*.

(B) THE CHOREOGRAPHER

The choreographer (clumsy word) *is the person who, guided by the music selected, arranges the movements of the dancers, creating that part of ballet which is danced.*

It is astonishing how mysterious this profession appears to the layman. Many who watch ballet for the first time imagine that the dances are improvisations; in other words, " just skipping about to the music," a phrase I have often heard. Even a learned judge and counsel in a recent case seemed to find some considerable difficulty in understanding the nature of the choreographer's art, and from various remarks that they let fall it was obvious that they considered it easy and of not much account, though they did eventually agree that it was susceptible to copyright. Actually, choreography is an extremely complex art, calling for exceptional knowledge, and the last fifty years have produced but a handful of choreographers whose work counts. Today, dancers and public in London, Paris, and New York rely on the work of Fokine, Massine, Nijinska, Balanchine, Lifar, de Valois, and Ashton. The first four in this list have been active a very long time; Fokine since the beginning of the century. The greatest problem in ballet is that of the lack of choreographers. The reason will be clear when I have analysed the art itself.

To start with, there is no school of choreography or recognised method of training. There could not be, apart from the higher education of dancers in general. The choreographer is a dancer with a strong urge to express himself, the good fortune and the ability to be able to do so. He is born and developed, but not made in cold blood. The present writer receives a score of letters every month asking how to become a choreographer. There is no reply, even when stamps are enclosed.

The first essential is to be an active member of a ballet company, so steeped in the classical tradition that the desire for self-expression arises almost as a reaction against routine. It is necessary to be musical and to have a practical knowledge of music. It is necessary to understand painting and sculpture, both historically and æsthetically. It is necessary to understand the mechanism of the theatre and the spirit of the theatre. It is necessary to have a knowledge of human nature, the ability to inspire confidence and loyalty. Your dancers are like the artist's tubes of paint, with the great difference that they must be both willing and receptive. Is it to be wondered at that the true choreographer is a rarity? I must make it clear that this rarity does not imply that choreography as an art is equal to musical composition or painting. The rarity lies in the fact that *the choreographer, by the nature of his work, is half-way between the creative and the interpretative artist.*

There are many who arrange dances. To do that requires a certain technical skill, but it is an entirely different matter. To arrange a dance merely means the fitting of the ready-made phrases (*enchaînements*) of dancing into a connected whole. That is within the province of the good teacher. Choreography itself implies originality of expression.

One of the difficulties of choreography is its impermanence. In the early days, when the main feature of ballet was its geometric pattern, it was comparatively simple to fix the movements in a system of script. Even when the technique of ballet became far more extended but ballet meant two or three persons actually performing with the *corps de ballet* as a decorative background, the problem was an easy one, especially as the music was simple in rhythm. The movements of classical ballet were restricted to a framework that it is possible to describe in words so that a dance could practically be transmitted by post. Although there are a variety of systems of script, not one of them is of much practical use to-day. Imagine attempting to reduce to paper such a ballet as *Choreartium*, where there is no *corps de ballet*, but a large ensemble of individuals, where but a few of the movements of those individuals can be described in words at all, and where the music is a symphony by Brahms! The very idea of such a combined score of motion and music makes the head reel. Nijinsky, in the first throes of his madness, grappled with such a problem. The film alone could come to the rescue, a film that could analyse in slow motion, and already the cost of ballet is prohibitive. *Giselle* and *Swan Lake* survive on paper, but the modern ballets run the grave risk of complete annihilation. They exist only in the

memory of their performers, and in this lies the strength
and the weakness of the art. Some central bureau for the
recording of ballet subsidised by the various companies
seems an essential in the near future; a task perhaps for
ballet's own museum, *Les Archives Internationales de la
Danse* in Paris.

It is comparatively easy, by adopting some set of standards of the type I have outlined, to judge the individual
dancer; extremely complicated to judge a ballet. There
are so many factors to be considered. We must know
something of the ballets that have gone before, and it is
not always convenient to study several repertoires. It is
impossible to form a very definite opinion, save of an
obviously wretched work, except after several viewings.
The musician will hear rather than see, the artist will study
the grouping, the dancer the steps and their execution.
For the average person it requires many visits to bring all
these together. We can talk here only of essentials, and
see later how they have been treated in a series of type
ballets.

The first essential, that postulated by Noverre and reiterated by Fokine, is consistency of plausibility. Ballet
is a convention, we have seen that from our definition.
The word need not disturb us. All the art that surrounds
us has its particular conventions, which for the most part,
through extreme familiarity, we accept unquestioningly.
Perspective in painting is a convention, the convention that
the two-dimensional has three dimensions; the bronze bust
is a convention, and we are not upset by the fact that the
human head and shoulders are gold, chocolate, or green in
colour. The theatre has its conventions. We accept a play
as realistic in spite of the fact that there is no fourth wall
and we have no right to be looking in on the drama. The
cinema has still more conventions, accepted by the millions
who are ignorant of the word and its meaning. It is possible to be moved by the plot of an opera or operette, if it
is skilfully presented. When you go to the ballet you

admit ballet's own particular conventions, but you demand from the producer that he himself respects them and is thoroughly consistent in his use of them. In *Le Spectre de la Rose* you are moved by the young girl returning from her first ball and beginning to day-dream and then to dream in her chair. The fact that no young girl just back from a dance actually settles down to dream to music does not for a moment disturb you. When her dream, the rose she has been given, comes to life and dances with her, you are moved by the poetry of the conception and you believe in what you are seeing. It has a truth of its own. But if that selfsame rose, instead of dancing lightly through the room, were to perform a vigorous Russian dance, you would be horrified and immediately lose your interest. The producer would, in fact, be a liar. This is not an extreme case by any means. Ballets equally ridiculous have been produced, ballets in Oriental or Greek settings where dancers have twirled on their toes. You do not demand accurate Oriental or Greek dances; doubtless, if you saw them, you would not recognise them. But you do demand something that does not shock your common sense. You know that a houri or a Greek maiden did not wear ballet slippers. You would be prepared to accept such a thing only in a highly stylised work that made a virtue of extreme artificiality, imposing yet another convention. You would then be entertained rather than moved. The essential difference between ballet and opera, on paper so similar by analogy, is that opera continually offends through the figures of the singers: mountainous women dying of consumption, ugly women assuming the role of *femmes fatales,* fat head-waiterish tenors aping ardent young lovers. A part of Chaliapine's greatness was the truth he brought to opera.

Another essential linked with this is theatrical quality. Ballet which tells a story is a play which, as Noverre has told us, must unfold itself logically. Ballet is extremely limited in its choice of subject. Once it has found a suitable subject, that subject is susceptible of a variety of interpretations, actual and symbolical. It is possible to convey the fact that X loves Y, X hates Y. Then X may be Mars and Y Venus, X Mammon and Y Money, Power, and so on. The language of ballet is both restricted and extended. It is quite impossible to convey that X is Y's sister-in-law, and if the plot hinges on that fact, then the ballet is a failure. "There are a quantity of things," said Noverre, "that cannot be rendered intelligible through gesture. Everything that one terms quiet dialogue is unsuited to Pantomime."

The choreographer, therefore, must choose only a theme that is suitable for his medium, and he cannot rely on the programme synopsis to save him. The ballet must be complete in itself.

Another essential that is immediately obvious in every other art is that the choreography must be the expression of a definite personality. It is personality, as we have seen, that distinguishes choreography from the arrangement of dances, however skilful. To judge of the originality of a work it is necessary to have had considerable experience.

The choreographer must use movements that his company can perform to perfection. It is useless to compose a work that calls for a succession of steps that only one exceptional individual can perform, or that the dancers can succeed in but every few performances. A good ballet is susceptible to a variety of changes of cast. The disturbing idea that the dancers may not be able to fill the choreography is immediately destructive of all illusion.

Good choreography must not, however, be interesting only because it presents an interesting story, it must be interesting bit by bit, in itself, through the use of the technique itself. Classical ballet, as we have seen, stresses line and purity of execution rather than literary conception. All ballet must be interesting in line and pattern. The dramatic content is one thing, the composition another.

The choreographer is a painter with a foreground, his principals, and a background, his *corps de ballet*. This is an exact parallel, but it cannot be carried any farther. It is comparatively easy to arrange effective groups. The choreographer's task consists in carrying the dancers from group to group. He is, in fact, painting thousands of different pictures, as a rapid camera will reveal. Each one of those pictures must in itself be harmonious. That is the essence of choreography.

To sum up, as far as we have gone, we have the following essentials: plausibility and a respect for truth; a subject that can be conveyed in pantomime; something original to say; a practical knowledge of technique; interest through the use of technique; a knowledge of composition.

These requisites are hard enough, but I have yet to tackle the core of the problem: the music.

(C) The Music

Music in ballet can fulfil a variety of different functions. It can be the servant of choreography by merely accompanying movement, its most primitive use. It can be the master of choreography by setting the choreographer a problem, how best to devise movement that will interpret or parallel its thought. It can be the equal partner of choreography in which composer and choreographer jointly deal with a problem. It has been all these things. In the earliest days of ballet it is the equal partner: the choreographer is usually himself a musician. Then it degenerates into a mere accompaniment, a conception akin to the jungle tom-tom, or earlier still, the clapping of hands and the stamping of feet, the dancer providing his own accompaniment. The choreographer designates a tempo, the composer obliges. With the advent of Isadora Duncan and in the early Diaghileff period music is the master. The music is already written, the composer dead, and the choreographer must fit his movement to what exists without permitting himself any liberties.

Diaghileff's ideal was to restore the equal partnership of music and choreography, which he did in *The Firebird, Petrouchka,* and a whole succession of works.

At the present time music is alternately the partner and the master. Since the success of the symphonic ballets, usually the master.

It is impossible to lay down any hard-and-fast rules. Successful ballets have been created under each one of these systems. It is certain, however, that music composed for a definite purpose should in theory give the best results. Ballet is a whole in which the ingredients must be carefully balanced. Whatever the system adopted, it is essential for the choreographer to have a subtle and highly trained musical sense.

The question is often asked whether all music is suitable for dancing. There is a wrong viewpoint, survival of the notion that ballet is frivolous: that certain music is too sacrosanct to be touched. It is not a question of sentiment, but of fact. Much music, by its structure, is quite unsuited for the dance. A dancer cannot perform a solo of more than a very limited duration; the music may call for mass action where the story calls for a solo, and so on. In using already-composed music there is a double risk: fitting a theme to it, fitting movement to it. Only in the case of the simplest or most formal music is this possible, or in music that has what Lambert, in an interesting essay, calls the quality of present action. Certain evocative music narrates and is physical, another type imagines. These distinctions are as real as direct and indirect speech, if less easy to define. However, the musical purist is apt to forget that ballet is theatre and must be judged by theatrical standards, and often his censure is true on paper, untrue in fact. I will discuss the subject of the symphonic ballets later. There is an interesting question as to the legitimate use of music in the case of *Le Coq d'Or.*

Le Coq d'Or was put on by Diaghileff in 1914 as an opera-ballet. The singers were stationed in the wings, the dancers held the stage and acted the plot. In this particular case it would be difficult to imagine a more successful presentation. *Le Coq d'Or* was revived by de Basil in 1937. Fokine, who had arranged the choreography of the original production, took charge of this, with the difference that the score was especially arranged by N. Tcherepnin, a pupil of Rimsky-Korsakov, the composer, as a ballet. The singing was entirely cut.

The work, with its magnificent costumes and scenery by Gontcharova, was unquestionably a theatrical success, but certain critics attacked it on musical grounds. They denied the right of anyone to modify a composer's music after his death. On moral grounds they were undoubtedly right. On practical grounds only partially so. They stated that music composed for the voice could not be adapted for the dance, that the adaptation injured the music itself and was in any case unsatisfactory.

Fokine's reply was interesting. While it did not directly answer the charges, since in a sense they are unanswerable, it posed fresh charges.

" The libretto of Rimsky-Korsakov's *Coq d'Or*," said Fokine, " is based on a wonderful play by our great poet Pushkin. In adapting it the composer took many liberties with the verse. We must not forget that *Le Coq d'Or* is Pushkin's as much as Rimsky-Korsakov's. In my dramatic form I am restoring much of the atmosphere and characterisation of the play." In other words, he is telling the musicians *Tu quoque*.

There were other arguments advanced, clever debating points, but they do not affect the main issue.

Undoubtedly a counsel of perfection would have been to commission fresh music round the same theme, but in practice the difficulties would have been too great. *Le Coq d'Or*, 1937 version, did offend musically, certain passages lost a great deal in value, and on that account alone it cannot rank with the choreographer's greatest. But it was a highly effective theatrical spectacle, and it did less artistic violence than a performance of the same work exactly as it was composed, but sung by fat singers with no conception of acting. In this last case, however, no musical critic would have objected, and in viewing ballet the musical critic is not always consistent.

The choreographer must have a musical conscience, the musician must understand that ballet is theatre, and often, for purely practical reasons, a compromise is necessary. This is no defence of musical vandalism, but a plea of mitigating circumstances.

(D) DÉCOR

We can best realise the function of scenery and costume in the entity that is ballet if we imagine performances of any of the works with which we are familiar in practice clothes and in front of plain curtains or a cyclorama.

Let us take a number of examples, starting with the romantic *Les Sylphides*, the very title of which makes us think of a dress worn by Taglioni, the direct inspiration of the work. Something would certainly remain, since the movement is beautiful in itself, but that movement was conceived with a special dress in view. The whole atmosphere of the enchanted grove would be lost. The gliding of sylphs would become the daily classroom exercises of flesh-and-blood young girls.

We can see from this simple example that while something of ballet still exists without costume (nothing remains without music or dancing), costume is not merely a pleasing embellishment added to the structure, but is a part of the structure. History has shown us the intimate connection between costume and dance. In this case it intensifies the atmosphere from a dramatic point of view. The same ballet danced in the revealing classical *tutu* would immediately distort the whole conception by drawing the spectator's attention to the physical side of the dance, muscle and virtuosity.

The fact that the same movement in different costumes

can convey such opposite impressions is a very striking example of the rôle that costume plays, and will aid us later in refuting a current fallacy. Our next example, *Les Présages*, is equally striking, and it has on one occasion been performed in practice costume. Yet, in spite of the fact that the way in which it is dressed is banal in the extreme, on that occasion the work lost a great deal of its meaning. The young lovers still made their effect, but the more positive character rôles degenerated into exercises; Fate was no longer menacing, Frivolity was agile but not truly gay, Action lost in strength. These costumes were not good, but they contributed something vital to the theatrical effect.

In neither of these examples have I mentioned the actual scenery. There is a difference of function between costume and scenery. Scenery is something physically apart from the dancers and is less indispensably connected with the whole. It can save a weak ballet, almost spoil a good one, and add the finishing touch to a great one. Its primary function is to form a background that will show up the line and the subtleties of the choreography. In the first scenic version of *La Symphonie Fantastique* the backcloth was dark and the dancers sombrely clad. A highly complex piece of choreography worked out in its smallest details was entirely lost. The second backcloth was light and revealed the richness of the detail. It failed, however, to help the atmosphere. Had it done so, it would have been a complete success.

Another example is that charming ballet, *Jeux d'Enfants*. Here the story is vague and has little significance on paper, but is strictly logical in action with a truth of its own. Its logic is irresistible because action, music, and scenery move in the same direction. The décor here shows the valuable contribution that surrealism can bring to the theatre. Remove the painter's contribution and the " truth " of this ballet would vanish.

The drop-curtain so frequently used must be properly

understood in its relation to the work. It must not be merely an enlarged picture. It is a part of the theatrical illusion. If it is too violent or restless, it destroys the mood. It must create a sympathetic atmosphere and also induce concentration. It is parallel to the musical overture.

We have deduced the following: costume is very closely linked with the actual choreography itself, since it is physically a part of the dancer. Costume intensifies the atmosphere dramatically and so assists the narration. Décor must show up the detail and pattern of the choreography. Décor must parallel the music and movement.

This is a refutation of the easy idea that costumes and décor are merely an embellishment. Yet today, since the death of Diaghileff, nearly all ballets are mounted on that principle. Music and choreography are settled first of all, then the painter comes in and dresses the result. The painter has the right to be a partner from the beginning. Not only must the choreographer know the shape of the costumes, but also their colour. If grouping means anything at all, it is obvious that colour plays as great a role as line. Painter and choreographer are as closely related as choreographer and composer, and painter and composer are also related through the choreography as well as through the subject-matter. Only through such a basic conception will really great ballets be created. It is impossible today to touch *Petrouchka, Carnaval*, or any of the major Diaghileff successes. To re-dress them would be to destroy them. But most of the recent successes would actually gain by a change of décor, a confession of weakness.

A partial definition of ballet from another angle might be helpful. *Ballet is the result of a collaboration in which musician, painter, and choreographer interpret a common subject, each one in his own medium; the closer the collaboration, the better the result.*

Historically, the evolution of décor has followed very similar lines to that of music. At the start it is so much a part of the dance that it practically dictates the movement. The early choreographer, if he does not devise his own costumes, is capable of exercising a very close control. Then it degenerates into a purely mechanical embellishment from which Diaghileff rescues it. Today it is well-meaning, but usually misapplied through lack of time and thought.

The early choreographers, Beauchamps, Noverre, Vigano, Blasis, were the men of exceptional knowledge in every branch of art. When the *maître de ballet* began to specialise in movement to the neglect of the other arts, it became necessary to replace his function of selection. It is this role that Diaghileff fulfilled so outstandingly. If décor today can be called well-meaning in principle, it is because Diaghileff educated every choreographer with whom he came into contact. Ballet décor is still entrusted to the interesting artist and not the professional theatre designer of pre-Diaghileff days. What is lacking is the authority to guide the right artist once he has been discovered. Once more we are up against the old problem, the education of the dancer, and with every fresh confrontation it strikes us as being more serious, until we are forced to the conclusion that when all dancers can only dance, ballet will be in immediate danger of extinction.

(E) Literature

According to our original definition, ballet expresses *an atmosphere, a theme, or a story*. It is clear, therefore, that literature must play an important role, and the more precisely that the exact nature of that role is understood, the better the ballet will be. A false literary conception at the start must kill the best of work.

Before the music is composed or chosen the ballet exists as an idea. That idea is the common meeting-ground of the musician, the choreographer, and the painter. It is easy to generalise and to draw up some elaborate theory that will look well on paper, but it is better to deduce our theory from the actual practice. Daily I receive intricate scenarios for ballet; a few of them might possibly be suitable as subjects, yet without fail they are entirely worthless. No ballet scenario submitted from the outside has ever received consideration, and for a very excellent reason.

The modern ballet according to the Diaghileff system is not based on a concrete scenario. It is based on a vague idea that grows, develops, and takes form through contact with the painters, musicians, and choreographers who are familiar with the medium. Literature does not dictate the form of the ballet. The immediate pre-Diaghileff method was to devise a scenario, like the plot of a play, and fit it with action, music, and costume. In the end, all that remained of the scenario was the story in the programme and some mechanical mime inserted at intervals. Words have a definite meaning, music and movement have not. There must therefore be a compromise, the nature of which will be evident when we select a few examples. I have already touched on the subject in the section on acting.

Petrouchka, the most successful of all dance dramas, had its origin as follows. Before undertaking *Le Sacre du Printemps,* Stravinsky wished to compose a work for piano and orchestra. " In composing the music," he says, " I had in my mind a distinct picture of a puppet suddenly endowed with life, exasperating the patience of the orchestra with diabolical cascades of arpeggi. The orchestra in turn retaliates with menacing trumpet blasts. The outcome is a terrific noise which reaches its climax and ends in the sorrowful and querulous collapse of the poor puppet. . . . I struggled for hours to find a title which would express in a word the character of my music and consequently the personality of this creature. . . . One day I leapt for joy. I had indeed found my title—*Petrouchka,* the immortal and unhappy hero of every fair in all countries."

This is still far from being a ballet. Then Stravinsky played it over to Diaghileff. " I played him the piece which I had just composed and which later became the second scene of *Petrouchka*. He was so much pleased with it that he would not leave it alone, and began persuading me to develop the theme of the puppet's sufferings and make it into a whole ballet."

With Diaghileff he gradually elaborated a story. Then Diaghileff wrote to Benois: "You must make the ballet which Igor Stravinsky and I have in mind. Yesterday I heard the music of the Russian Dance and Petrouchka's shrieks which he had just composed. . . ."

Benois had always been interested in fairs, and so gave the ballet its setting, inventing the figure of the old charlatan from the inspiration of his favourite Hoffmann.

Accounts vary as to how the final story was arrived at. Actually, it was a close collaboration between the composer and the painter, each one of whom understood the medium of ballet, and of the choreographer Fokine, who brought final reality to their dreams.

This is typical of ballet creation, the translation into something concrete of a visual impression and not of a written synopsis.

There is the case of *Le Sacre du Printemps,* also revealed to us by Stravinsky in his valuable memoirs. "One day, when I was finishing the last pages of *L'Oiseau de Feu* in St. Petersburg, I had a fleeting vision which came to me as a complete surprise, my mind at the moment being full of other things. *I saw in imagination* a solemn pagan rite: sage elders, seated in a circle, watched a young girl dance herself to death. They were sacrificing her to propitiate the god of Spring. . . . I must confess that *this vision* made a deep impression on me, and I at once described it to my friend Nicholas Roerich, he being a painter who had specialised in pagan subjects. He welcomed my inspiration with enthusiasm and became my collaborator in this creation. I told Diaghileff about it, and he was at once carried away by the idea. . . ."

I have italicised certain words to stress the visual origin

of the idea. Nijinsky was also groping for a theme that would free him from the eternal use of purely classical technique, and so *Le Sacre du Printemps* was created.

Still one further example, this time of a very definite narrative to music already composed and for another story.

The origin of *Scheherazade* is still under dispute, and for the very reason that it was a perfect collaboration. Prince Lieven, relating Alexandre Benois' point of view, writes: "Diaghileff hit upon the idea of producing a ballet to Rimsky-Korsakov's *Scheherazade*. . . . As a youth Benois had heard and enjoyed this music, and for some reason he had associated it in his imagination with the prologue to the *Arabian Nights*. . . . Rimsky-Korsakov's music was written to quite a different programme. . . .

"The conferences of the friends about ballet generally followed these lines: the music was played until it had induced in the listeners some *plastic image*. . . . He (Benois) would fall into a sort of trance, shout to the others to keep quiet, and begin abruptly, accompanied by the music, to relate the appropriate ballet."

It would appear from these accounts that the original idea of a ballet that grows into a narrative is arrived at by accident. That is not altogether correct. The persons to whom the ideas arrive and by whom they are developed are practical men of the theatre, soaked in the atmosphere of ballet and thoroughly conscious of the medium.

When ballets have been conceived by men of letters, those men have been poets, and poets in the *entourage* of the ballet. Théophile Gautier visualised the story of *Giselle* after reading Heine; Jean Louis Vaudoyer visualised *Le Spectre de la Rose* after reading Gautier. Jean Cocteau, who devised many ballets, is a painter as well as a poet-dramatist; Boris Kochno, a poet and an expert theatre man. The majority of the recent English ballets have been devised by the composer Constant Lambert, musical director of the Sadler's Wells Company. There is no exception to the rule that the scenario devised in a purely literary manner is worthless. The actual workers in ballet must be fired with enthusiasm by some plastic image that is discussed and rediscussed until it takes on a definite form. To start with a definite form is to court disaster. Sometimes the ballet remains vague: *Les Sylphides*, the atmosphere of a sylph-haunted wood; *Carnaval*, the coming to life of Schumann's musical images; *Cotillon*, a ball with certain vague and mysterious happenings; *Jeux d'Enfants*, the fantastic secret life of toys; *Rendezvous*, greetings, partings, and flirtations. In such cases music has suggested the atmosphere. In others it has been colour. But always it is the artist who has created the literary element of ballet.

(F) Economics [1]

This is a strange, forbidding section to be found in a chapter on the æsthetic background of ballet, but the economic situation affects everything that we have been discussing so strongly that it belongs here: the ghost at an æsthetic banquet. However interesting it may be to dream about the ideal ballet under ideal conditions, it is a pure waste of time not to take into consideration things as they actually are; also, it is unfair to those who are having to contend with such conditions. The expenses of ballet production are so heavy that no one directly connected with its production receives an adequate reward, however great the success. Its origin at the court of a wealthy monarch is a thing to remember at all times.

To start once again with the dancer: an ordinary English girl, who has none of the benefits of a State institution. The budget varies considerably, but I have taken a fair average from a number submitted to me: underestimating, if anything.

During the ordinary school-age period, from eight to fifteen, she will take about two classes a week during eight months of the year: average cost of the class, 4s. Total cost, £43 16s., excluding shoes, practice dress, etc. It

[1] The figures quoted here refer, of course, to peace-time conditions.

would be fair to rate her dancing education for those seven years at £50.

From fifteen to seventeen years of age, she will take a lesson a day for eight months of the year at £1 a week. In addition she will probably pay £12 a year on a series of private lessons. This makes the cost of the last two years £88, with no extras for dress. Total cost to turn out a dancer, £138 to £150.

By that time she is, according to modern usage, ready to join a company. Thousands of girls pass through dancing class every year; of those, one hundred may have the ambition to join a ballet company. There are some three companies with perhaps six vacancies altogether, and it must be remembered that the Russian companies have the schools of the entire world to supply their wants. They have more offers than they can consider, even of girls wishing to join under apprenticeship conditions. It is clear that the candidate, to be successful, must have altogether exceptional gifts and also exceptional luck.

Once she is chosen for the *corps de ballet* she may be paid, on an average, £5 a week. She will be given a pair of shoes for every eight or twelve performances: it depends on the custom of the particular company. This is inadequate, and she will have to purchase about three extra pairs a month at an average price of 6s. a pair. In addition she must provide her own tights—silk—at £3 3s. a pair. With luck a pair may last a year, but she will need to keep two pairs going. Her expenses are not yet fully met. There is her make-up, which comes to about £4 to £5 a year. Not very much remains to reward an exceptionally talented girl for work that is nearly as hard as that of a hospital nurse. Also, most girls take classes at their own expense in addition to those given by the company. There is, of course, the possibility of a rise in salary and position. With exceptional good fortune it could reach £15 a week. In such a case the dancer would be almost at the top of her profession, as well known to her followers, though they would be smaller in number, as the actress earning £40 a week, or the featured film player earning from £150. Not a very bright picture.

The dancer must have a very genuine vocation, as well as some private means behind her. If she is dancing in London and living with her parents her situation is much better, but in a Russian company she will be travelling and keeping herself for about seven months of the year.

From these figures it would look very much as if the dancer were being exploited. Such is not the case.

Let us now look at the business budget. It is not possible to give exact figures, since there are great differences in company budgets. Here is a rough indication. The orchestra is protected by union regulations; if the dancer was also, there would be no ballet at all. An orchestra may cost anything from £500 to £700 a week. Extra rehearsals of a complicated work will run the bill way up. I can remember one bill of £1,400 for the week. There is the stage staff, union wages with extra for overtime; the front of the house staff, the electric light bill, the publicity, advertising, and printing. These may fall to the lot of the theatre engaging the company or upon theatre and ballet manager in a proportion arranged by contract. The theatre may guarantee the manager so much per week and a percentage of profits. The manager's own expenses are enormous. Firstly, his salary bill and general running costs, including copyright on certain works—anything up to £7 a performance—and renewals of costumes (perspiration not being conducive to a very long life). He will have to pay an agent a booking fee of ten per cent. on his guarantee and over. For some extraordinary reason there is often more than the one agent. Ballet attracts hangers-on who dip their fingers into the profits. Then there are the production costs. A theatre manager will expect three new ballets during a season. A new ballet will cost anything from £750 to £3,000. The idea of the music, and its execution, band parts, and rehearsals, must be paid for;

the conception of the scenery and costumes and their execution must be paid for, as well as various extras in entertaining during the launching of a new work. The new ballet accounts for only one-third of the evening's entertainment. It will pay its way only if it is good enough to take its place in the regular repertoire, and so be played over a number of years. Even then it may not in itself be a box-office draw, but may please patrons once they are already in the house. To be a box-office draw it must have absolutely extraordinary merit. The majority of Diaghileff's early ballets have amply paid for themselves, though he did not see the profit, wiped out by too many extravagant ventures. A failure may run for half a dozen performances and then be fit for the scrapheap. Under these circumstances—and the picture is not unduly gloomy, but is drawn mainly from experiences with very successful companies—it is not surprising that the dancers are badly paid; indeed, it is surprising that they are paid at all.

We have not yet reckoned with the expenses of travel and the wear and tear of travel. The public for ballet is still comparatively small. The fact that there are many who come night after night deceives us as to the exact number. Apart from London, which gives by far the best returns and can support a company for about three months with a repertoire of twenty-five ballets, there are few cities that can support more than a week. This means that constant travel is an absolute necessity. Experience shows that if a company rests for more than a month in the year, its artists disperse. They badly need the holiday, but cannot afford it. The sphere of travel in Europe is greatly restricted by political and economic questions. The pre-war ballet map of Europe consisted of England, Monte Carlo with an odd week in Italy, Germany, and Scandinavia. Ballet has rarely paid well in France. The world map includes America, Australia, and South Africa, with South America a possible market, but difficult at the moment. Journeys must obviously be long; two Atlantic crossings a year, all of which must be financed by some-one.[1]

Agents and impresarios gain when things are going well; the ballet itself rarely has money to spare; everything must be immediately reinvested.

This picture explains many artistic shortcomings in an art that was never intended to be commercialised. It explains the eagerness to utilise existing music, out of copyright, and also the inability to find time in which to develop the education of the dancers. Every counsel of perfection must be weighed against the actual state of things. At the same time sound artistic planning, invoking the principles I have discussed, would in the end prove both good art and sound business, if one can use such a term about anything so precarious as ballet. The successful struggle of ballet from the luxury of a court to the rough and tumble of constant travel, while it has affected its æsthetic, shows the essentially healthy condition of the art.

(G) THE MAKING OF A DANCER—IN PRACTICE

Since we have left the rarefied atmosphere of æsthetics for the consideration of economics, it might be well to continue this chapter on a practical note.

I receive hundreds of letters every year from anxious mothers asking how their daughters are to be made into *ballerinas*. I can never reply by anything very positive and likely to please an anxious mother, not through unwillingness, but because I cannot speak without a knowledge of the prospective *ballerina*—and of her mother. In a country where there is a State institution there is no problem at all. Here, the parent must use considerable judgment, and also, in the creation of an artist, the home atmosphere

---

[1] The case of Sadler's Wells is entirely different and resembles in many respects a State institution. It is subsidised to the extent of a remission of entertainment tax and a guarantee from C.E.M.A. On the other hand, it plays at popular prices and only twice a week, so that its position is not altogether easy.

counts for a great deal. Here is a summary of the only advice I have been able to give.

1. Is your daughter really well built: not too tall (five feet six inches is the beginning of the danger-point)? Is she strong and healthy?

If she is not well built, by all means let her study dancing. Careful teaching will improve her physique; but let her take up dancing with no illusions of a career, though there have been cases where knock-knees or bow-legs have been remedied in an extraordinary manner by a teacher who understands anatomy.

If she is delicate, consult your doctor, but experience shows that dancing is healthy. A career in ballet under modern conditions requires exceptional health.

On no account let her go in for slimming. If the hard work does not reduce her, then the cause of the fatness is probably glandular. Hard muscular work needs plenty of sugar as fuel. It is the mother's task to adapt routine and diet to the conditions of work. In England, where a ballet career is comparatively new and is a private matter, scarcely anything is understood about a dancer's health, which ruins more careers than any other single factor.

2. Do not neglect the rest of her education, particularly music. Piano is a definite asset to a dancer, and should be a part of her education.

3. Do not stress examinations or become a cup-hunter, for reasons obvious in the text of this chapter. Examinations are only of value when properly understood, and are better taken late than early.

4. Once you have found a teacher whose record, academic and theatrical—and I believe in a teacher with a practical experience of the stage—impresses you, trust her and do not interfere or move the child from school to school. There are mothers who send their unfortunate daughters to three or more schools: unfair to everyone concerned.

5. Do not expect rapid results or be disappointed if she

does not dance from the very start. The important thing is the correct placing of the body, upon which everything depends. This takes time, and nearly all present-day dancers are made to dance too soon; either because it flatters their parents' vanity, or because it is a pressing financial necessity. It is nearly always impossible to eradicate the mistakes of a false start.

6. Round ten is the correct age to start; before eight it is positively harmful. Over twelve the pupil is a little handicapped, unless she is naturally supple and athletic. Over sixteen it is too late to hope for a successful career.

7. Always bear in mind that dancing is not merely something physical and apart from the pupil's reactions to everyday life. Character is revealed in movement to an extraordinary degree, as any psychiatrist will reveal. Meanness, arrogance, untidiness, shyness, fear, self-indulgence, slyness, lack of discipline are all traits that are speedily revealed in the dance. Therefore the parent has as much control of the pupil as the teacher and can touch certain springs hidden to the teacher. Often the parent undoes the excellent work of the dancing school, through imagining that the budding genius requires very special treatment, instead of a thoroughly normal disciplined life on common-sense lines. I know of numberless examples, which every teacher can confirm, of good material ruined by misplaced affection.

The mother should not sit and watch every movement of the class, as so many do. It would be equally ridiculous to watch the son's geography or Latin lessons. The same point of view applies to each case.

The ballet mother has been notorious for the past hundred years. Albert Smith, author of an amusing pamphlet published in 1857, *The Natural History of the Ballet Girl*, writes: " The Ballet Girl has more frequently a mother than a father; a singular provision of Nature appears to have denied the latter parent to them. . . . But they have all got mothers. . . ."

8. I have outlined the economic aspect of making a dancer. In cases of exceptional talent, the really good teacher will make considerable reductions. A successful pupil is her finest advertisement. Also there are various scholarships available.

9. To join a company requires perseverance, patience, exceptional ability, and good fortune. If you aim at a career in ballet for your daughter, you must be an idealist, for a ballet career in the ordinary course of events is not a practical aim. The openings are too few and the rewards too small.

(H) Outlets: Ballet Clubs, Examinations, and Competitions

One of the most recent and most important developments in this country has been the spontaneous formation of ballet clubs by *balletomanes,* teachers, and their pupils. These clubs put on shows periodically (shows that are more than the ordinary pupil displays because they are the result of collaboration), arrange lectures, discussions, and debates. The shows may often be indifferent, judged from professional standards; no matter. The value lies in the will to create and in the opportunity that hundreds of girls are given to have some contact with the stage.

Today the average girl works chiefly for exams, those of the Royal Academy of Dancing and other bodies. These exams are carefully arranged, but in practice they can be as harmful as they can be beneficial. They do not as yet sufficiently distinguish between pupils who are learning to be teachers and pupils who have stage ambition. Teachers must have certain qualifications, and the Royal Academy and kindred bodies have done admirable work in granting their certificates only to those who have satisfied the examiners. Such certificates cannot assure good teaching, but they can guard, as far as is humanly possible, against bad teaching, and they can make it almost impossible for the charlatan to earn a living. However, all pupils do not aim at becoming teachers, and examinations are apt to give an entirely wrong angle to the would-be *ballerina,* stressing technique at the expense of stage-craft. The whole system needs a drastic revision. I have seen many pupils who have passed advanced examinations and who are quite incapable of dancing, though they can perform steps. This is the rule rather than the exception. The ballet club movement, once it has spread and been developed along the proper lines, can give the pupil who has stage ambitions a really valuable experience and compensate for the eternal examination grind.

This is no attack on the examination principle in general —all State academies recognise its value—but a plea for its revision in a way that will distinguish between the stage artist and the teacher-to-be. A State academy aims at turning out dancers and can arrange its education and examinations accordingly. The fault of the present system is that it is working completely in the dark and solely from the point of view that the main aim of the pupil is to teach. If this is so, then the future of dancing is in a bad way, for the best teachers must have had a preliminary stage experience. The ballet club movement once harnessed can provide this, and in time should prove a dominant factor in English dancing life.

Another outlet for the pupil, the only creative one before the formation of ballet clubs, has been the competition. This can be admirable, if properly applied, but all too often it degenerates into pot-hunting. The work done at the local ballet club can teach certain values that will make competition work of far greater artistic value, and the ballet club organiser can watch the competitions closely for choreographic as well as dancing talent. It should be the bridge between examinations, competitions, and the actual ballet stage. In this way it will prove the best friend of both teachers and pupils.

Another important aspect of the ballet club movement is as a propagandist force. It can create a public, make its local press look upon ballet as news, and in this way make it possible for companies to increase their touring field, which will in its turn fill the schools and increase the ballet club membership.

The formation of ballet clubs all over the country, and their affiliation into a group that can ensure a certain artistic standard, are the next steps that ballet will take in this country. Its accomplishment will more than compensate for the lack of a State-supported organisation.

CHAPTER 4

Makers of Modern Ballet

(I) SERGE DIAGHILEFF

The reign of an absolute monarch

(I)

THE history of ballet is continuous: it travels from country to country, Italy to France, France and Italy to Russia, Russia to England; but it remains in the hands of those who have inherited the tradition. There is evolution but never revolution; progress is gradual and not forced. It is difficult to judge where exactly the history of modern ballet begins. I left my historical survey with the advent of three foreigners—Petipa, Johannsen, and then Cecchetti— to Russia. The effect of that arrival truly starts the story of modern ballet as we know it in practice today.

Petipa, a Frenchman from Marseilles, had a unique opportunity in which to found a school, having charge of the same company for some fifty years and mounting on them fifty-seven full-length ballets in all as well as super-vising all the work that was done. Neither Noverre nor Blasis, superior in every way as thinkers, had such a chance to exercise and develop his craft.

As a teacher Johannsen enjoyed similar opportunities, bringing with him the pure French school which the French themselves were beginning to forget. Soon there was a whole generation of Russian-born dancers, where formerly they had been exceptions.

Work under one *maître de ballet,* however gifted, over a long number of years becomes monotonous, and after a quarter of a century Petipa was beginning to work by formula. The dances themselves were also getting into a groove when the Italian Cecchetti appeared in a private theatre with an Italian company. Grace and elegance were a characteristic of the French, strength and virtuosity of the Italians, and it was their virtuosity that appealed to the public. Greatly daring, the then director of the Imperial Theatres, A. Vsevolojsky, engaged Cecchetti as a *maître de ballet.* Cecchetti was a teacher of genius. The new Italian method plus the rivalry caused by the two schools brought something new and vital, giving birth to a Russian method, *three-quarters French school and a quarter Italian school seen through the Russian temperament and shown through the Russian physique.* That is the exact meaning of that much-abused term *Russian Ballet.* English Ballet about to be born as a method will consist of the Russian school seen through the English temperament and shown through the English physique. It is already beginning to take shape, too embryonic as yet to characterise and label in the inexactly exact manner so beloved of critics.

In addition to engaging Cecchetti, who supplied the ingredient missing in Russian Ballet, Vsevolojsky commissioned ballets from Tchaïkovsky, interesting after a very long interval the original musician in the medium of ballet.

But in every art a period of great perfection gives way to a sterile academism. A Raphael and a Michelangelo arise, leaving behind both beauty and an impossible path to follow. Their genuine personal discoveries become laws, the form of their work is followed but not its spirit. And they must wait fresh discovery at a later period when criticism allows them to be valued afresh. The formula of their work is repeated when its meaning is no more. Sometimes a veteran seeks to repeat his own early successes with the same result. Petipa was a veteran. By 1900 he had served the theatre fifty years, accomplishing a gigantic task. His work, thanks to the wise guidance of Vsevolojsky, had undergone one renaissance, but he had reached the end. Though ballet had never reached the low ebb of France, had never degenerated to the music-hall, as in England, there was nothing in it of interest for the thinking man. The conservative *balletomane* sat in his front row, peered and applauded, criticised, compared, and applauded. He did not wish for a change; he, too, had become a somewhat quaint survival. Ballet and *balletomanes* were museum exhibits.

There were great dancers who often shone in works unworthy of them—Kchesinska, sparkling virtuoso outstanding in *Esmeralda;* the perfectly classical Trefilova; Preobrajenska, witty, and the idol of the gallery; Egorova and others. While Pavlova travelled, they earned the plaudits of the *balletomanes* at home.

The renaissance of dancing has been theirs. As *émigrées* forced to spend their retirement teaching in Paris, they have formed the whole present generation of Russian dancers.

Isadora Duncan came to Russia and caused a sensation. She wore the flowing draperies that Sallé had vainly attempted to introduce two centuries before. She discarded the ballet shoe, sacred symbol of the art of dancing. More daringly she danced to music that had been heard only in the concert-hall and that the majority of the *balletomanes* were quite incapable of understanding. She tried to interpret the meaning of that music in her dances. Technically she was a revolutionary, artistically, as we know, she was returning to the first principles of ballet.

She expressed herself as horrified by the artificialities of ballet, she praised and patronised individual dancers. Her advent would have made little permanent impression had others connected with the academic body itself not felt exactly the same.

Michael Fokine, a graduate of both the Imperial and dramatic schools, a musician and a painter, was undergoing a process similar to that of Duncan. He was not a revolutionary in her sense, for he valued the tradition and the training out of which he was born and wished to preserve what was best. His aim was to resume where

Noverre and Blasis had left off. Duncan was horrified by what she saw, and illogically blamed the whole art for the manner in which it was being used. Fokine approved of the basis of the art, but wished to find a different application in which nature could become once again the guiding inspiration. She objected to the use of the points in dancing, he to the abuse of the points. She and her followers exaggerated their importance just as the ballet was doing.

His first step was to abolish the enormously long entire evening ballet. To him, ballet must express itself with economy, not pretend to tell a story and then proceed to ignore it. Theme, atmosphere, correct style were the things that truly mattered. His first ballets, *Nuits d'Égypte* and *Eunice,* while they earned the admiration of the wise old man, Petipa, caused such an uproar that they nearly drove him from the theatre. Here was the tradition that they had established with such care and expense being destroyed by a young upstart. But it was he who understood the true tradition, not they. The fellow was actually making *ballerinas* dance on their bare feet and upsetting the sacred order of things so completely that one could no longer tell at what period in the ballet the " high spot " of the evening occurred. These were indeed infamies, said the ballet Blimps.

Fokine might have abandoned the dance altogether if artists in other media had not been following a parallel path and did not see in ballet the perfect medium for the music and art in which they were interested.

(II)

The leader of this group of earnest young thinkers was Alexandre Benois, a man of encyclopædic knowledge in every branch of art and literature, the descendant of a long line of artists, painters, and architects. His maternal grandfather was a composer, his uncle a distinguished theatrical architect.

As a student at school he had already gathered round him a group of friends, and later, at the university, they formed themselves into a club in which each one lectured on his own particular subject.

It is a characteristic of Russians to discuss endlessly until they have ·talked the original subject completely away, preferring dreams to reality, and Benois' group might easily have done the same, though Benois himself was a creative artist, had it not been for the advent of Serge Diaghileff, a country cousin of one of them.

Serge Pavlovitch Diaghileff was born at Perm in 1872. He belonged to the country nobility, an important factor in discussing his character. His environment was one of ease and culture, in which music and theatricals played a large part. It was his ambition to become a composer, but he came to St. Petersburg to study law at the university.

From the first he was different from the little group surrounding Benois. They considered him to be definitely provincial, less cultured than they, and, in spite of that, a little too bumptious and aggressive. They were definitely smug. He did not at first belong to the inner circle, he was on the fringe of the group purely through the accident of cousinship.

His university career was a secondary consideration. He went to the theatre, the opera, and to concerts, and developed his music, though early on he met with a check when Rimsky-Korsakov told him that he did not have an original talent. He is said to have retorted with supreme self-confidence, " I will be remembered when you are forgotten." He did much to make Rimsky-Korsakov remembered. He travelled, visited studios and museums, and in conversation with friends sharpened his critical faculties. He was an enthusiast able to communicate his enthusiasm. Soon he became the leader of the group, the man who could put their theories into practical reality.

It was natural that with so much to express the friends should turn to journalism, and under the editorship of

Diaghileff and Benois they started *The World of Art* (*Mir Isskoustva*). The difficulties of the undertaking were enormous. Russia was behind-hand in artistic book production, and it was necessary to find the plant from abroad and to create the journal physically as well as artistically. This and the organisation of a series of art exhibitions proved Diaghileff's abilities as an active organiser, and taught him the first essentials of an *impresario*, though the term describes only a small part of his true function.

The platform of *The World of Art* was individualism. " One of the greatest merits of our times," wrote Diaghileff, " is to recognise individuality under every guise and at every epoch." He defined art as a " free and disinterested act taking place in the soul of the artist." " The sole function of art is pleasure, its only instrument beauty. . . . It is blasphemous to force ideas."

He maintained that art should exist for art's sake and not to teach a practical lesson. It could have no concern with earthly difficulties. He attacked both didactic art and sterile academism, making himself a host of enemies.

(III)

It is only natural that with such a reformer's platform, ballet should appear as an ideal medium and one in which the quickest results could be obtained. They had within their own group the necessary painters and musicians, and the young choreographer Fokine was burning for an opportunity to express himself.

During his first years in St. Petersburg Diaghileff was not interested in ballet, seeing only the ridiculous artificialities that had it in a stranglehold. Benois and his friend Nouvel, through seeing an exceptional dancer, Virginia Zucchi, were the only confirmed *balletomanes,* and it was they who turned Diaghileff's thoughts in that direction.

The friends seemed to have gained their opportunity almost without a struggle when Diaghileff was offered an administrative post in the Imperial Theatres by a director eager for reform, Prince Serge Wolkonsky. Both through the journal and his conduct of the theatre Diaghileff had made many enemies. He was complely uncompromising. The production of Delibes' *Sylvia* was to be entrusted to him when those enemies revolted and, addressing a deputation to Wolkonsky, refused to have anything to do with the production. Wolkonsky, faced with a strike, countermanded the production. Diaghileff insisted and was dismissed. A year later, Wolkonsky himself resigned after an administrative dispute, and the key post of director of the Imperial Theatres fell into the hands of a reactionary, Teliakovsky, an avowed enemy of Diaghileff and the group. All hopes of successful experiments in ballet in Russia were dead.

Diaghileff continued to organise exhibitions with great success, brought Russian painting, music, and opera to Paris, but never ceased to dream of ballet.

Finally, in 1909, after conquering innumerable difficulties, many of them provoked by his own uncompromising attitude, he brought a Russian company to Paris, where its success revolutionised the history of ballet in Western Europe and later in America, leaving only his own country out of it, until today in Russia, country of the successful revolution, the tradition of Petipa continues almost unchanged, though a commissar may sit in the box of an Emperor.

(IV)

To understand the character of the new Russian Ballet it is necessary to understand the character and artistic evolution of its founder, for the ballets he presented were the expression of his artistic tastes of the moment. Save with Gautier, and Gautier's influence was far less, there is no one who can be compared with Diaghileff, non-dancer, non-composer, non-artist, who influenced the ballet, the music, and the art of his whole period.

The first conception we must have is that of the noble-man. The Russian noblemen had their own troupes, who performed for their pleasure and for that of their friends. Diaghileff was the direct descendant of such serf-owning nobles, and it coloured his attitude. He was first of all a man who indulged his own personal tastes and graciously allowed his friends to share his pleasure, and only afterwards a business man interested in such prosaic affairs as the box-office. Today the box-office must rule and we can no longer look at the ballet in the same way. Diaghileff represents the bridge between monarch and business man. Only after him does ballet become truly democratic.

Though Diaghileff was an autocrat he never attempted to dispense with advisers, and he had the flair for discovering new collaborators throughout his career. We have examined the ingredients that compose ballet, and since nowhere does the role of a Diaghileff appear, one must ask oneself exactly in what it consisted.

He created the role, it was a part of his mental make-up. He was a Mæcenas who did not spend his own money, an impresario who ignored the public taste, a business man who lost money; all these are negative things. As he never wrote or talked about himself we must deduce the positive ones. I have asked the majority of his collaborators to enlighten me, and their usual reply is a vague one that assigns to him some organising role or other and leaves the creative side to them. This is not so much a question of jealousy as of ignorance. They were the medium in which Diaghileff worked. Someone in his *entourage* would suggest an idea at supper, the idea would appeal to him. He would think of a composer and painter and introduce the idea to them. They would discuss it, with Diaghileff there to prompt and encourage them, then in a few months' time, in some cases a few years, a ballet would be ready. By that time no one could say whose was the original idea, and there was no trace of Diaghileff's work; but it was he who prevented the idea from being swept away with the remains of the meal and who found the very people who could develop it.

Once it had become a production, his function became that of censor. Before he had acted through flair, now it was through knowledge. He criticised music, both the composition and the execution, and musicians listened to him with respect and the minimum of anger. He modified a costume, suggested a change in the colour scheme, and so on. The dancing alone he did not touch, but he influenced the choreographer during the months in which the work was in question. Added to his flair was a passion for education. He discovered a "genius," a word that he was fond of using, then took him to museums and concerts, brought him into contact with artists, moulding his opinions and trying to mould his character. So that, even though his name appears on no programme opposite a specified function, every production bore the imprint of his personality. The one role which he readily admitted was that of lighting expert. He had an extraordinary knowledge of theatre lighting and endless patience, spending as much as twelve hours on a set, until he had reached perfection. Today, it is all done within an hour, and unfortunately all too often conveys that impression. The essence of a Diaghileff production was its unity and the close attention to minute detail, at times extravagant and unnecessary.

His taste varied, as we shall see when we discuss the work, over the years, and there seems a contradiction at times between the cosmopolitan who was a patriot, the lover of Tchaikovsky, who belonged to the *avant-garde,* the romantic, who showed us *Le Pas d'Acier*; a contradiction that has raised doubts as to his sincerity. There is not the space here to trace bit by bit the happenings of his private life and their influence on his work; also it is not within the scope of this book. The one important thing to note is that it can be done and that it shows beyond doubt that the Diaghileff Ballet was Diaghileff.

Diaghileff was all his life terrified of death, admiring intensely everything that was young and vital. It is that quest for youth, growing feverish as he advanced in years, that accounts for the frantic modernism of the last phase, and all the time there was a deep natural love of the classicism and romanticism that reminded him of his own youth and the resultant conflict between the two. That is the only way in which we can truly understand Diaghileff.

Much has been written about his brutality and the manner in which he treated Nijinsky. This does not concern us here, though it must have altered the course of ballet history. An art such as ballet, where the tradition belongs to but a few people at one time and in one place—and during the twenty-five years the living art of ballet was travelling with Diaghileff, a part of his baggage—is constantly being influenced by private relationships. Diaghileff was domineering: no mild-mannered man could have kept the company alive throughout the 1914 War; but some of the portraits that have been painted of him as a scheming, mediæval villain are ridiculous and not borne out by facts, which show that he was loyal to his collaborators, with certain exceptions, throughout his long reign.

He was no Svengali, and those collaborators were neither mediums nor puppets, but thinking, intelligent beings, the finest artistic minds of the age, whom he stimulated and inspired: a different matter altogether. A type of legend has grown up, books, films, and plays have seized upon it, and history has been grossly distorted as a result. It is easier to believe in a legend than to investigate hard facts. My concern here is not to do justice to Diaghileff, but to trace the development of ballet with accuracy.

(v)

From ignoring Diaghileff's role altogether to exaggerating it and ignoring that of his many collaborators is an easy step. Diaghileff started his career under the strong influence of Benois and with a choreographer, Fokine, who was already formed. Before the start of the company Fokine had produced *Nuits d'Égypte*, afterwards *Cleopatra*, *Chopiniana*, afterwards *Les Sylphides*, *Carnaval*, and, under the influence of Benois, *Le Pavillon d'Armide*. Diaghileff improved the detail of these works, had the Chopin and the Schumann re-orchestrated; but in this first phase his function was purely that of censor, propagandist, and impresario.

(*a*) *Music*

The characteristic of this first period of a year, 1909, is the use of adapted music. The Diaghileff Ballet begins to be a fully creative artistic force with the collaboration of Stravinsky the following year in *The Firebird*.

" Throughout the winter," writes Stravinsky, " I worked strenuously at my ballet, and that brought me into constant touch with Diaghileff and his collaborators. Fokine created the choreography of *The Firebird*, section by section, as the music was handed to him. I attended every rehearsal with the company, and after rehearsals Diaghileff, Nijinsky, and myself generally ended the day with a fine dinner, washed down with good claret."

The significant phrases here are the *constant touch* and the *fine dinner*. It was on such informal occasions that Diaghileff worked, and the close association resulted in a whole series of ballets: *Petrouchka*, 1911; *Sacre du Printemps*, 1912; the ballets that made the name of Stravinsky and that interested the serious musicians in ballet, a hitherto despised art.

Stravinsky collaborated with Diaghileff till the end, not merely as a composer, but as minister of music to the cabinet. As soon as sufficient composers had become interested, no more ready-made music was used, though music was frequently adapted with marked success in such ballets as *Pulcinella*, *La Boutique Fantasque*, and *Les Dames de Bonne Humeur*.

Today, there is no minister for music in the Russian

Ballet cabinet, and the young composer is beginning to abandon ballet. One of the reasons for the artistic success of Sadler's Wells is that Constant Lambert, trained in the Diaghileff *milieu,* has assumed that function.

(b) Décor

The décor of the Diaghileff Ballet was fully creative from the very start, under the guidance of Alexandre Benois. *The World of Art* had aimed at reforms in painting, and one of the reasons for the founding of the ballet was to give the new painting a platform. The artists concerned in the first decorative period from 1909 until the first year of the War were Russians: Benois, Bakst, Roerich, Korovin, Gontcharova, with the modernist Larionov as a bridge between the modern French painters and the Russians.

While Benois outlined the policy it was Bakst, with his glowing, exotic colours, who attracted the attention and who revolutionised the decorative art of the world. The change in decorative policy was brought about by two reasons—the accident of war that separated Benois and Diaghileff (Bakst remained a collaborator till the end of his life), and the quest of Diaghileff after novelty. He was always frightened of degenerating into a formula, eager to go in advance of the public taste. Even without the War such a change would have come about, and he was already interested in the work of Larionov, a Moscow painter who had come under the influence of Paris. The æsthetic of ballet swung from the new romanticism to the grotesque, from curves to angles. It was a natural reaction from the arabesque to the cold logic of a Picasso, and Picasso and his followers took the place of Benois. The easel artist replaced the professional theatre artist, and in his turn became a professional, the same evolution as in Russia itself. The essential thing to remember is the close collaboration throughout. Monte Carlo, where the ballet remained for some months in every year, was the G.H.Q. at which the artists in every medium met and exchanged ideas. Today, without that close contact with the theatre, the easel artist is apt to remain a complete amateur. Throughout the life of the Diaghileff Ballet, when music and choreography declined, the décor remained on an exceptionally high level.

(c) Dancing

During its first years, until 1910, the Diaghileff Ballet remained a travelling branch of the Imperial Theatre, the dancers joining Diaghileff during their long vacation. There was only the difficulty of finding appropriate dates. When, after the *Giselle* scandal,[1] Nijinsky was dismissed from the Imperial Service, Diaghileff formed his own company and the artists were faced with a choice, but until the War the supply of highly trained dancers was unfailing. After Pavlova's defection Diaghileff found in Karsavina an ideal *ballerina*: a woman of exceptional intelligence, in thorough sympathy with the new movement, and with a range of expression that made her available for every role. For a long time she continued a dual existence as a *ballerina* at St. Petersburg, interpreting the classics, as the standard-bearer of the new ballet. Karsavina remains the ideal of the modern *ballerina*, with every attribute that I have outlined, and it is with her in mind that I have set my standards.

Closely associated with her is Vaslav Nijinsky. He has become a legend, and it is difficult to write about legends. He was the first Russian male dancer to be seen in Western Europe; memory plays tricks, and how much greater he was than any other dancer since it is impossible to say. He was clearly a great instinctive artist, to whom technique was a servant.

Among the other artists of this great dancing period were Lydia Lopokova, later *ballerina* of the company, Lubov Tchernicheva, a strong dramatic actress fortunately

---

[1] See *Diaghileff*, by Arnold L. Haskell.

still on the stage, and Adolf Bolm. But all were experienced in stage-craft and finished dancers of a type that belongs to the past. Among them was one exceptional English girl, Lydia Sokolova, whose musical knowledge and dramatic ability made her definitely one of them.

Diaghileff never at any time wished to alter either the type or the training of his dancers. His ideal was the pure classical *ballerina.* When war and revolution separated him from the great manufactory of *ballerinas,* he tried to reproduce the system abroad, engaging maestro Cecchetti for the classics and the intensive training of especially talented dancers.

Vera Nemtchinova became his first *ballerina* not trained in the Imperial schools who had risen out of his own ranks. The fine Polish dancers, Idzikovski and Woizikovski, played an important role, stressing the invaluable work of Cecchetti in Warsaw. Many English dancers joined the company, among them Vera Savina, light, and of exceptional elevation, who made a great reputation, Ninette de Valois, Alicia Markova, and an Englishman, Anton Dolin, who became *premier danseur classique.*

Diaghileff engaged the strictly classical Olga Spessivtseva when he was able, Ludmila Schollar and Anatol Wilzak, magnificent *danseur noble,* and induced Vera Trefilova, the purest of all the classicists, to return to the stage, but almost imperceptibly a change was coming about. During his last three years the bulk of the work was entrusted to three highly talented but immature and not yet fully trained dancers: Alice Nikitina, Alexandra Danilova, and Serge Lifar, all of whom made names at a much later period. The programme could not be revealingly classical, and the modernist experiments did not assist in the training of the young dancers. It was a vicious circle. The period of the wonder children trained by the St. Petersburg *ballerina émigrées* in Paris was still five years distant.

(d) Choreography

Until the 1914 War, with but a brief interregnum, Fokine was in charge of the choreography. It is interesting to note that out of thirteen works of his produced during that period eleven still survive, and *Les Sylphides, Carnaval, Prince Igor,* and *Petrouchka* are the most constantly given of all ballets. *Fokine is, beyond all question, the father of contemporary ballet, and his works are school pieces in the sense that they must be studied by everyone connected with ballet.*

The interregnum of 1912–1913 was brought about through personal reasons, but the ballets of 1914, *Papillons* and *Joseph's Legend,* seem to show that Fokine was a little weary and inclined to repeat a success without success.

Nijinsky's ballets, with one exception, *L'Après-midi d'un Faune,* do not survive today. He was undoubtedly a greater dancer than choreographer; a man with something very definite to express, but without the means, the necessary musical knowledge, of expressing it. The constant contact with pure classicism seems to have inspired in him a revolt in which he wished to express strong primitive things in a jerky, angular fashion as far removed from the Fokine ballets as possible. The first attempt, *L'Après-midi d'un Faune,* caused a first-rate scandal, being attacked by the *Figaro* on moral grounds and defended by Rodin on æsthetic ones. This was followed by *Jeux,* a tennis ballet, which was a complete failure, and *Le Sacre du Printemps,* which provoked a still greater scandal. The Nijinsky legend must not blind us to facts. Stravinsky says of *Le Sacre du Printemps*: " Nijinsky began by demanding such a fantastic number of rehearsals that it was physically impossible to give them to him. It will not be difficult to understand why he wanted so many, when I say that in trying to explain to him the construction of my work in general outline and in detail, I discovered that I should achieve nothing until I had taught him the very rudiments of music. . . . When, in listening to music, he contemplated movements, it was always necessary to remind him that he must make them accord with the *tempo,* its divisions and values."

The Nijinsky interregnum, however, was of value, even if the work was not. It shook the dancers from their composure and prevented the Russians from adopting a formula of success, and in similar fashion it shook the public and made them watch attentively. It is all too easy to take in alone the more obvious beauty of ballet, to watch it in a sort of trance and to ignore its character. The sudden shock of these scandals prevented that. The true enrichment of ballet and the movement away from neo-romanticism was brought about by Leonide Massine. Nijinsky paved the way.

Leonide Massine started his career as a soloist in 1914, and as choreographer in 1915. *He still dominates the stage in both capacities, one of the outstanding figures in the whole history of ballet.*

With Massine the Diaghileff Ballet begins a new phase; it is truly the Diaghileff Ballet, while during the first few years the Diaghileff-Fokine Ballet would be a more accurate description.

When Nijinsky left the company Diaghileff was faced with finding a successor to dance the role of the young Joseph in *Joseph's Legend,* an ambitious ballet commissioned from Richard Strauss. The work of a very young man in the Moscow school attracted his attention and he engaged him. From the first Massine showed unusual ability, taking advantage of the immense educational facilities given him. He devoured books, studied in museums, and listened to the conversation of artists. It was immediately obvious that this was to be no ordinary dancer. In accordance with the new tendencies of the ballet, Diaghileff entrusted a large part of his protégé's early artistic education to Larionov.

The first ballet, *The Midnight Sun,* a pagan Russian festival in a grotesque setting by Larionov, was produced in 1915 at the Opéra, Paris, for a War charity gala. It is still in the repertoire today, a slight work, but one that already reveals an extraordinary gift for the use of folk material. This was followed by some Spanish fragments, the education for *Three-cornered Hat,* and by a portion of what became *Contes Russes.* The influence of Larionov was still great. With his first full-length ballet, a masterpiece, *Les Dames de Bonne Humeur,* Massine became completely himself, producing ballet after ballet until he left in 1921. There could be no question of replacing him, no risk of his discovering a formula. He was infinitely varied, deeply interested in experiment. Following on Fokine's reforms and Nijinsky's unfulfilled ambitions, he greatly enriched the pattern of the dance, bringing to it the dances of Spain, the inspiration of Hogarth and Callot, the cubism of Picasso, and the spirit of the machine age. His invention is far from exhausted, he is the major figure in the contemporary ballet. At his worst he exaggerated movement in compositions that reminded one of the later Raphael, a phase that soon disappeared when he was no longer caught up in the modern movement and began to look back to classicism as a firm foundation. Massine left Diaghileff in 1921 for purely personal reasons, only to return later as a guest.

The fact of Massine leaving, as well as a sentimental memory of his youth, turned Diaghileff back to classicism. In an age of democracy he decided to present a lavish revival of the famous Maryinsky ballet: Tchaikovsky's *Sleeping Princess.* As usual, he prepared the ground with great care. The music was partly re-orchestrated by Stravinsky, who reassured the moderns that this was no retrograde step, that Tchaikovsky was the most characteristic of all Russian composers, and that they must not be deceived by the traditional Muscovite flavour absent in his music. The ballet was dressed and decorated by Leon Bakst and additional numbers from *Casse-Noisette* were incorporated into it. Diaghileff engaged the last of the classical *ballerinas,* Vera Trefilova and Olga Spessivtseva, for the role of Aurora, and greatly enriched his company. As a sentimental gesture characteristic of the man he engaged Carlotta Brianza, who had created the role in the original production, to mime the wicked fairy Carabosse.

The result was the first truly classical Russian ballet on a grand scale that London had ever seen, and consequently the first opportunity to gain a real basic knowledge of ballet. For a quantity of reasons a work that would have enjoyed success today was a comparative failure.

Diaghileff was expected to provide surprises, but of a Left tendency, and in spite of his skilled propaganda he could not counterbalance a propaganda of the past. The man who had presented a cubist manifesto, *Parade,* was not expected to return to the æsthetics of his ancestors. His public was comparatively small, and not one that understood the finer points of ballet. The fashion was against him, and for once in his life he could not sway it. The work was very extravagantly produced, requiring a year's run to show any profit. A mechanical device went wrong on the first night and ruined an effective scene.

Diaghileff's lesson had its full effect only in retrospect. It undoubtedly set a standard of dancing.

The immediate reaction of this failure, which endangered the very existence of the company, was to make him turn to modernism once again. His new choreographer was Bronislava Nijinska, sister of Nijinsky, and a very remarkable dancer. Nijinska turned to choreography through necessity. She was teaching in Kiev with the ambition of forming dancers to interpret her brother's ballets. She saw that the orthodox curriculum was inadequate, and her first attempts at choreography consisted in exercises for her pupils. Through that departure she became the most personal of all choreographers, teaching the dancers first of all to think in terms of her work. For Diaghileff she produced one masterpiece, *Les Noces,* to Stravinsky's music,

misunderstood in this country but warmly defended by
H. G. Wells. *Les Noces* was a ballet of intricate mass
movement that revealed the esoteric meaning of a Russian
peasant marriage. Her other ballets were ingenious satires,
works which by their outlook denied them permanence.
The Blue Train, created for Anton Dolin, showed the use
of acrobatic technique with a classical ballet plastique. It
was a satire on the frequenters of the Riviera, handsome
athletes, golf and tennis champions, and bathers. *Les
Biches*, with music by Poulenc and admirable interpretative
scenery by Marie Laurencin, was a vicious commentary on
a group of modern nymphs, ladies of pleasure, and their
reactions when three handsome athletes entered their estab-
lishment. It was disguised in England under the grossly
misleading title of *The House Party*.

Nijinska has been unfortunate in her ballets. The
Diaghileff material denied them the permanence that their
choreography demanded. Later, she did magnificent work
for Ida Rubinstein with *Bolero, La Valse, La Bienaimée,
Les Noces de Psyché et de l'Amour*, seen only for a few
weeks. For her own very short-lived company she produced *Les Comédiens Jaloux, Beethoven Variations*, and
Hamlet. All these works deserved a permanent company
to present them. Her influence on dancing, however, has
been profound. Lifar, Lichine, Dolin, Shabelevsky, Verchinina, Morosova, Ashton, and others all owe an immense
debt to her training.

When she left Diaghileff her place was taken by Georges
Balanchine, who came to him more formed than either
Massine or Nijinska. Balanchine, a pupil of the Imperial
schools and a fine musician, had begun to emerge during
the Revolution, but his work was considered too artistically
revolutionary for Russia and he left with a small group of
dancers. His ballets for Diaghileff came during a bad
period, and, though they caused a sensation, the public had
dwindled to a small and rather precious clique. The best
known were *La Chatte, The Gods go a-begging, Barabau*,

Apollon Musagètes, and *Le Fils Prodigue*, not one of which survives. They were ingenious and intensely personal distortions of classicism that promptly dated as none of the earlier Diaghileff ballets had done.

The last choreographer of the company was Serge Lifar. In Stravinsky's *Le Renard*, under the guidance of Larionov, master of the grotesque, he tried the interesting experiment of presenting movement done by both dancers and acrobats, but he lacked the necessary experience to get the most out of it.

This long experimental phase produced many interesting results, but on the whole it was based on the sensationalism that Diaghileff had learned from the scandals of the Nijinsky regime. In much of the work Diaghileff himself did not believe. He was frightened of old age and of being superseded, and was indulging in a mad chase after youth. These experiments would eventually have killed ballet. They ended just in time, and there is evidence that had Diaghileff lived he himself would have turned his back on them. His last performance ended with a magnificent revival of *The Swan Lake*, in which Spessivtseva, classical *ballerina par excellence*, shone.

The company held in it the seeds of the future. Lifar went as choreographer and *premier danseur* to the original home of ballet, the Paris Opéra, and has dominated the dance there ever since. Tcherkas went to the Opéra Comique. Balanchine and Grigorieff were among the founders of the de Basil Company. Ninette de Valois founded the Vic-Wells Ballet, and Markova and Dolin were its first stars. Massine is still the biggest figure in ballet today. The company as an entity died with its great founder, but so living was his inspiration that fragments of it took root all over the world and today dominate the whole movement. Bolm is settled in Chicago, Balanchine founded the American Ballet in New York, Nijinska worked in Buenos Aires, Nemtchinova and Zvereff went to Kovno. Everywhere the name of Diaghileff lives on.

He died in Venice in 1929, and his mortal remains lie buried there.

(II) ANNA PAVLOVA

(I) *An exception to the rule*

Outside of Russia Anna Pavlova was greatly misunderstood by the very people who should best have appreciated her art. Were she to return today she would gain a new and far more critical audience.

Such a statement about an artist whose name is to this day synonymous with dancing may seem a paradox. It is not.

Pavlova was seen and admired the world over, but largely by people who were not deeply interested in the art of ballet, who would flock to the Winter Garden Pavilion to see Kreisler one week, Harry Lauder the next, and Pavlova the next. They went into raptures at her daintiness, marvelled at the fact that she could dance on the points of her toes. They most certainly missed the essentials of her art, a fact that worried her in spite of her success. One very definite effect upon those audiences the world over, apart from a memory of beauty to light up a drab existence, was to determine them to have their daughters taught dancing. Schools sprang up like mushrooms in her wake. When I have asked countless dancers all over the world what made them start, the answer is more often than not: " Mother saw Pavlova," or " I saw Pavlova." There has never been so great a propagandist force for the art of dancing: England, the Dominions, the Colonies, America, Mexico, South America, Java, China, Japan all saw and marvelled.

The small clique of people who really enjoyed ballet, who could discuss it in an amazing technical jargon, stood aloof. To them ballet meant one thing alone: the surprises in music, décor, and choreography brought them yearly by Diaghileff. That and that alone meant ballet.

They had very little conception of dancing itself as a great interpretative art.

When I first met Pavlova she said to me: " Are you on my side or Diaghileff's? " At the time the remark seemed to me unnecessary and I could not grasp its significance. It was many years before I understood it clearly, after both Pavlova and Diaghileff were dead. There were sides and there should not have been; a proper understanding of the art, such as that of the great critic André Levinson, consisted of a balance between the two. Both Pavlova and Diaghileff were the architects of contemporary ballet. Had one of them alone been responsible the result would have been a leaning tower of Pisa; certainly a good deal less stable, ready to be destroyed by the first gale of criticism.

Pavlova and Diaghileff set out on the journey together. Pavlova was one of Diaghileff's main inspirations. He was to go to Paris to show this amazing product of Russian Ballet.

Diaghileff held modern views; we have seen the effect of the reaction on his group of what was being produced at the Maryinsky. Pavlova also was a rebel, a romantic who wished to escape from the pure virtuosity of classicism.

Pavlova was *The Dying Swan,* and Fokine's one-person ballet was truly a manifesto of the new choreographic outlook, difficult as such a conception may appear to us today.

Let us take the Swan Princess of *Swan Lake* and Fokine's creation. In the first the Swan was undisguisedly a *ballerina* who used the story to reveal her gifts as a dancer. If she was an outstanding personality and a dramatic actress as well, so much the better. She could make it more interesting than it actually was. *The Dying Swan* was never an excuse for pyrotechnics. In technique it was absurdly simple—any pupil could master the steps in a short time; but the steps were only the beginning, the means to an end, and the end was to interpret the atmosphere of the music and to convey a tragedy. *The Dying*

Swan showed the death of an ephemeral creature and not the prowess of a *ballerina*. As such, it was the manifesto of Fokine's new romanticism. At the start Pavlova's path, Fokine's path, and Diaghileff's path were identical.

(II)

Anna Pavlova was born in St. Petersburg, a weak and premature child, on January 31st, 1882. She was not expected to live. She was removed to Ligova, in the country outside the city, and the air soon proved beneficial. Her love of the country, her direct contact with nature, were to colour her entire artistic outlook, and many of her best-known dances are an interpretation of nature: *The Dragonfly, The Californian Poppy, Autumn Leaves.*

As a holiday treat she was taken to see a matinée of *The Sleeping Princess,* as so many children were to be taken to see her and with the same result. From that moment her mind was made up. Her mother took her to the Imperial schools, but to her bitter disappointment she was too young. Pupils were not received before the age of ten (a warning to the impatient parent of today), and she still had two more years to wait. During those two years her resolve grew still stronger.

When the time came, she had to face a dreaded test. There were about a hundred candidates, with only seven or eight vacancies, and a formidable jury of directors and dancers past and present. Health was an essential and Pavlova was still frail. It speaks well for the discernment of the judges that she was among those selected. The course took seven years and consisted not only of dancing but of an excellent general and artistic education. She was taught by A. Oblakov, the former *ballerina* Vasem, and an outstanding actor-dancer, Paul Gerdt, pupil of Johannsen. Gerdt took an enormous interest in his unusual pupil, teaching her in such a way as to turn her frailty into an asset. She finished her schooling at the age of seventeen with the high grade of " first dancer."

The later Valerian Svetloff, an enlightened critic, describes her début.

"I found myself in a cosy little corner, in the lighted, warm green realm of the dryads. This little corner was the Mikhailovsky Theatre and the dryads proved to be unreal, for they were represented by ordinary pupils of the theatrical school. . . .

"The jury sat in the front row, putting down marks to the dryads. This alone somewhat destroyed the illusion. . . .

"It was on this evening that for the first time the public saw the pupil, Pavlova, and it was on this evening that for the first time she attracted the attention of everybody. . . . With childish ingenuousness she acted a *scène de coquetterie* with a young peasant and with playful wantonness danced with the imaginary dryads. All this was youthfully gay and pretty, and nothing more need be said, except that the play of the child's features in the scene with the peasant was already full of expression, and one had the feeling that here was something individual, something that was not learnt by rote at school. But in the solo variation from *The Vestal Virgin* one already felt something more, something that made it possible for one, without posing as a prophet, to foresee in the youthful dancer a future great artist."

Valerian Svetloff, my master as a critic, followed this career step by step, outliving Pavlova by several years. May he rest in a heaven where Taglioni and his own beloved Pavlova for ever dance.

Pavlova continued for some time as a pupil, when already on the stage, learning in Johannsen's perfection classes. But one generation separated Johannsen from Vestris. Pavlova was of the real aristocracy of ballet.

Within a few years she had made an immense reputation, sealing it with her interpretation of *Giselle*. Her ethereal qualities, in striking contrast to the more robust strength of her contemporaries, awoke memories of

Taglioni and suggested a new romanticism. In 1905 she became a pupil of Cecchetti, adding something of Italian strength and precision to her frail grace. The dancer, unlike any other artist, is always a pupil even at the very height of her fame, and Cecchetti continued to be her master for many years. One of the greatest differences between the *ballerina* of yesterday and of today was the realisation that learning is never finished. The *ballerina* of today, once famous, has not the opportunity to increase her knowledge, even when she has the desire. Pavlova may have ruled her own company as a complete autocrat, but

there was always someone to whom she was the pupil in need of guidance and correction.

Pavlova's first journey abroad was to Riga in 1908, with a small company, and the following year she visited Scandinavia and Germany. It was the beginning of her triumphal campaign.

(III)

Her successes abroad played their part in deciding Diaghileff to undertake his adventure. Fokine, the chosen choreographer of the new movement, had found in Pavlova a true inspiration. "She is the greatest *ballerina* in the world, excelling both in classicism and in character. Like a Taglioni she doesn't dance, but floats; of her, also, one might say that she could walk over a cornfield without bending an ear."

So spoke Diaghileff to Gabriel Astruc one evening at Paillard's when the question of bringing Russian Ballet to Paris first arose. And Pavlova came to Paris to dance with the Diaghileff Ballet. Jean Louis Vaudoyer wrote of her: "Mademoiselle Pavlova is to dancing what a Racine is to poetry, a Poussin to painting, a Gluck to music." But, in spite of this praise from an exceptionally understanding critic, Pavlova was overshadowed in the press by Nijinsky in *Les Sylphides* and Ida Rubinstein in *Cleopatra*. Today, this seems difficult to understand. But in Paris in 1909 a male dancer was a complete novelty, and also Diaghileff was personally interested in launching his protégé. The "Biblical Rubinstein," who posed rather than danced and who was the centrepiece of a sensational scene, being unwrapped from her mummy clothes to appear in all her striking beauty, represented the exotic element expected from the Russians. Whatever the cause, this distribution of praise altered the career of Pavlova and with it the history of ballet. The first poster of the Russian Ballet bore her portrait, she was a part, a large part of the inspiration, but she left at the end of the first season.

This departure left behind a permanent trace of bitterness, and Diaghileff was never fair to Pavlova, going out of his way to extol an obviously inferior *ballerina,* comparatively speaking, at her expense. Pavlova clearly remained his ideal, hence the note of hostility when he said: "Pavlova was never really interested in art as such. The only thing that mattered to her was virtuosity, and she is a virtuoso without equal. When first I wanted her to do Stravinsky's *The Firebird,* especially designed for her, she declared that she wouldn't dance to such horrible music."

This estimate of Pavlova as primarily a virtuoso is patently ridiculous. She was never a virtuoso, and, judged by such standards, there were and are many far greater than she. She revolted against virtuosity in the same way as Fokine and Diaghileff himself had done. She was greatly interested in art, only her viewpoint began to differ, partly no doubt through reaction against Diaghileff.

She saw the art of ballet menaced by modern tendencies and rallied to its defence. The phrase: "Are you on my side or Diaghileff's?" was for her full of meaning, especially spoken at a time when he was on the extreme Left and she, as if to balance him, on the extreme Right. She danced for him once again as a guest artist during the coronation season in 1911. The rest of her career consists of voyages and triumphs right up to the day of her death.[1]

Diaghileff's æsthetic was a personal one, but expressed through the medium of others; consequently it was by its very nature more objective. Pavlova's was expressed through her own mind and body. She was surrounded by a company, but that company was a background and her whole balletic conception was subjective, whether this was her conscious aim or not. In fact, it was not, for she thought of ballet in the wider sense, even though the word was always spelt Pavlova.

Early in her travels the Russian and Polish members in her company came to blows, and she found it impossible to manage them. From this moment she deliberately filled her company with English dancers. Their docility was the first point in their favour. Later, their aptitude for the dance became more apparent. During her lifetime the Pavlova company was of no importance; when she died it became of outstanding importance. She had trained a whole generation. If they did not make a name as individuals, they became teachers and missionaries. The

[1] There are rumours of a Pavlova film; let us in the name of good taste pray that it never materialises. Her whole life was her art, and the dancer who essays the role will be ridiculous in the eyes of all who remember her. The fact that there is no possibility of an interesting scenario from such a life may not deter Hollywood, but the idea of a dancer aiding in such a fraud is utterly revolting.—A. L. H.

discipline she had given them and the type of girl that she selected proved that ballet was a possible career for the carefully brought up " daughters of gentlemen," and not an excuse for a life of frivolity. From both sides of the stage Pavlova's value as a propagandist cannot be over-estimated, and that propaganda continues as well as the inspiration of her art. What type of artist was she? What did she express and how does she fit into the history of ballet?

(IV)

It is best to begin with a physical portrait. I have already mentioned her fragility; it was only in appearance when she began her career, for she enjoyed robust health until the day of her untimely death. Physically, she was remarkable, with long, perfectly proportioned arms that accentuated the large movements so characteristic of the Russian school; exceptionally well-modelled legs showing none of the bulging, over-developed muscle so characteristic of many dancers; strong, slender ankles, and a highly developed instep as strong as steel. Her face was not beautiful in a conventional sense; it was interesting and it was the perfect instrument for her art. She could assume beauty at will: the wild beauty of the Bacchante, the exotic beauty of the gipsy, or the sweet prettiness of the girl in such a fragment as *Noël*. When she was no longer young and her face in repose betrayed some of the ravages of an exceptionally hard life, it would on the stage appear still young and almost girlish; not the result of make-up— I watched her often enough from the wings—but of artistry. There was very little difference between the young Pavlova and the Pavlova of the last few years. The head was beautifully placed on the shoulders. She moved with a natural grace, which teaching had accentuated, and many of her dances were dances of grace rather than show pieces. Her range was a wide one, combining both Taglioni and

99

Elssler; but she excelled in the portrayal of the pathetic, of some ephemeral being that came to life and then withered and died all on a summer's day.

Much has been written of her love of birds and flowers. Such topics are a joy to the press agent, but the birds are all too often caged and the flowers wired. In the case of Pavlova this close observation of nature and the identification of herself with nature has a very definite meaning. Her Swan, Dragonfly, and Poppy were not portraits in the exact sense of the word, but they were translations that could have been made only by someone who really felt in complete harmony with nature. What struck me the most about Pavlova was not just the fact that her dancing seemed entirely spontaneous, but that it seemed a natural phenomenon, like the ripple of a pond, the opening of a flower, or the leaves being whisked and whirled by the wind. Such imaginative descriptions may seem extravagant, especially in the English language, and they are used by a critic who usually mistrusts them profoundly, but they represent the only manner in which one can convey something of the impression created by Pavlova. It is, perhaps, because of this gift of appearing natural that one was inclined to take her for granted and only to begin to analyse her after her death.

It is always said that she rose above her material by what Benois has aptly termed "a theatrical miracle," that she danced the dances of every day as no one had ever done, and this is true. When she died a number of roles died with her. She was creative, for she had created these roles out of almost nothing; and even a great conception like *The Dying Swan* has become an impossibility without her.

But those phrases are also used as a reproach and must be examined from that point of view. The dancer is a part of a complicated organism, and her personality and artistry must not be allowed to become the sole *raison d'être* of ballet. There is no doubt that *Les Sylphides* was more worthy of her gifts than the indifferent *Chopiniana* in which she danced; that *The Firebird* is a living work of art where *Don Quixote* was killed at birth by its wretched music; that *The Fairy Doll* has no artistic justification. This is admitted, the whole trend of this book has been to explain and insist upon such facts. The Pavlova of a great work, *Giselle,* was the greatest Pavlova of all. While we accept this, we cannot blame Pavlova herself. There was and is no machinery into which she could be fitted. She had left the Maryinsky far behind, and after the first few years the atmosphere of the Diaghileff Ballet was a hostile one. We cannot see Pavlova even in such great works as *La Boutique Fantasque* or *The Good-humoured Ladies.* She was an organisation on her own as well as an individual; there were the Maryinsky, Diaghileff, and Pavlova. That is the important point to remember. Maryinsky and Diaghileff could continue, but Pavlova was as ephemeral as the beings she so truly interpreted. The machinery that grew up around her was, by its very nature, both temporary and a compromise. If we do not remember her, it will not bear critical examination. There was nothing more pathetic than the few performances of the Pavlova Ballet without Pavlova. This machinery, however, was worthily conceived. She could as a concert dancer have attracted the masses. People, in any case, came to see *The Dying Swan* rather than anything else. It is a tribute to her conscience as an artist that she realised that only in a large *ensemble* could she really shine. There is no truth in the supposition that jealousy prevented her from appearing with other great artists. She may or may not have been jealous, but she outshone her generation and had nothing to fear. She shone alone against a drab but worthy background, because she was an exception to every rule and it is impossible to fit a lasting framework round an exception.

Her importance in the history of ballet and as one of the founders of the contemporary movement lies in the fact that she proved to the world that the ballet dancer could be a completely expressive artist, the equal of a Duse, a Bernhardt, or a Chaliapine. She stands as an ideal and an inspiration, and her value as an influence lives on after her.

The phrase " Pavlova as an ideal and an inspiration " must not be misunderstood, as it so often is when people ignorantly talk of " a second Pavlova." Had Pavlova been a second Taglioni she would never have made an impression. She was the first and only Pavlova. There may be equally great dancers in the future, not reflections of Pavlova, but fresh personalities. The machinery that produced a Pavlova has been broken by economic conditions, but true genius will find a way.

The only manner in which to understand Pavlova as an ideal is to understand her attitude towards her art and the true extent of her accomplishment. She started with lavish natural gifts and she transformed them into conscious artistry, ceaselessly learning and perfecting what she had been given.

CHAPTER 5

Personalities of Contemporary Ballet

(I) COLONEL DE BASIL

Limited monarchy and contemporary Russian Ballet

(I)

COLONEL DE BASIL will never receive full credit for his remarkable achievement in popularising ballet. The legend of Diaghileff will always intervene. Yet no two men could have been more different in personality, aim, method, and achievement. There can be no direct comparison.

The ballet from 1909 till 1929 was always, as we have seen, the expression of Diaghileff's personal tastes; the season's programme depended upon his enthusiasm of the moment, and he was consistent in his enthusiasms. He was still very much in spirit the lordly owner of a private troupe. Detail of production was to him all-important. De Basil is far more impersonal. He is interested in reaching as wide a public as possible; in the general effect and not the perfection of detail. Where Diaghileff took a year or more to conceive a ballet, de Basil takes a few months or even weeks. The choice of work does not depend upon his inner artistic urge.

These marked differences give us an opportunity of surveying contemporary Russian Ballet. The change from Diaghileff to de Basil was nearly as great as the change from Imperial Stage to Diaghileff; Emperor, nobleman, simple man of action.

We can best appreciate both the situation and de Basil's role by examining the economic position. In the Imperial Theatres ballet was a pampered hothouse flower, denied nothing to make it flourish. Diaghileff brought it out into the open, but gave it the same care as is given to the flowers of the Casino garden at Monte Carlo. De Basil has made it perfectly hardy, able to survive in the frozen north or the Middle West. Under Diaghileff ballet was never financially self-supporting. He first evolved an idea, regardless of cost, and then found the money from his entourage of wealthy backers. Under no circumstances did he modify a scheme. The Imperial Theatre made a feature of lavish production; by their standards Diaghileff's ideas were simple, but of the masterly simplicity that costs money. The dress was not ready-made; just because of the simplicity of its cut it had to come from the finest *couturière*. It is quite futile to speculate as to what would have happened had Diaghileff lived. The economic crisis would have made an enormous difference to his method of working. He disliked compromise. De Basil was the type of man that the Russian Ballet needed at that moment, and he succeeded beyond a doubt. Under de Basil for the first time in history repertory ballet became self-supporting. This meant the necessity of appealing to a world public, and of taking into account what that public wanted. In doing so de Basil saved the ambulant ballet, and no comparison with Diaghileff can be allowed to rob him of the credit. He had vision and courage. In its artistic detail ballet may have suffered, but on the whole the first years of de Basil were artistically healthier than the last rather weary and disillusioned years of Diaghileff.

It is interesting to consider the problem that faced de Basil. To the world at large, ballet was one individual of genius, Anna Pavlova. To a very small coterie of artists it meant the aspirations of another individual, Serge Diaghileff. The death of Pavlova meant that the masses no longer had an interest in ballet; the death of Diaghileff, that the artists and patrons were openly hostile to any attempt at forming a company. "Diaghileff is dead," said a French critic; "with him all the fairy-like images of his teeming imagination have become but memories." They called him "ce prodigieux animateur," wrote reams about the glories of the Russian invasion of 1909. They did not analyse his achievement in a critical spirit, and they did not for a moment think of the art itself that had started at the court of their own Louis XIV. They were writing the obituary of ballet.

It is fatal to think of an art solely in terms of an individual, and the effects of that mistake had first of all to be overcome by de Basil. In Paris he has never completely overcome it. He succeeded, because he is essentially a fighter, because he did not attempt to continue the Diaghileff tradition, and through the help of René Blum at Monte Carlo and certain of the Diaghileff artists who were not defeatists.

De Basil was not a theatre man by profession. He was a colonel of a Cossack division, a soldier with a distinguished war record. Of that there is no doubt, though his detractors have even sought to deny it. In any case, it has no bearing on his theatrical life. After the usual hardships of emigration, he started a theatrical and concert agency and a small troupe of dancers that was more or less a family affair. He even took part in it himself. Next, he became a director with Prince Tseretelli of the Russian opera, coming to the Lyceum in 1931. The opera gave a few evenings devoted to ballet. These were indifferent, but they revealed the public demand and were his first lessons in running a company. He left the opera to concentrate on ballet. Diaghileff was dead and he was alone in the field.

With René Blum, director of the theatre, he formed a troupe for the Monte Carlo season. Balanchine, Diaghileff's last choreographer, worked with him, as well as the experienced stage director Serge Grigorieff, in harness since 1909. The main problem was the personnel of the company, and there he made a bold decision that assured his success. The Paris studios of the great Maryinsky *ballerinas,* Preobrajenska, Kchesínska, Egorova, Trefilova, who had settled down to teach after the Revolution, contained a group of child prodigies. These thirteen-year-olds differed considerably from the previous generations of

Russian dancers. Suffering had given them a precocity unknown to their carefully cloistered elders. It had given them a close contact with humanity. Also, compared to their predecessors, their training was perfunctory, but two factors gave them exceptional technical facility.

Teaching had made extraordinary progress, and they were being taught by the most experienced dancers of their day; also the modern girl is physically stronger and more of a natural athlete than the corseted girl of pre-War days. These children were able to perform feats of virtuosity that had rarely been attempted before.

The *fouetté* is a case in point. More than anything else it made the popularity of the new ballet. The public is always over-susceptible to virtuosity. The *fouetté* was first launched, if not invented, by the Italian, Pierrina Legnani. In the third act of *Swan Lake* her series of thirty-two caused a sensation, eager *balletomanes* counting aloud, as if it had been an exhibition of athletics, which in many respects it was. The sensitive critic found it out of place in this romantic ballet, though, in fact, there was a slender dramatic justification, since the bewitched girl is meant to dazzle the Prince by her brilliance. For a long time no Russian could emulate Legnani, until finally Kchesinska found out the secret, amidst national rejoicing. Even then, it was by no means universal, neither Pavlova nor Karsavina adopting it. This rare trick of the multiple *fouetté*, not properly in the dancer's repertoire, became a commonplace to the young dancers of the emigration. They could perform thirty-two, sixty-four, and more, if necessary, and they did it with ease and precision. It was now no more a trick but a part of the current language of dancing, and as such, the choreographer could use it expressively to tell his story and not to surprise the audience. We have in a previous chapter seen the slender division between dancing and acrobatics.[1] The first ballets in the de Basil repertory all contained *fouettés*, and the

[1] See page 41.

fouettés entranced the audience, gave the critics something
to discuss, and launched thirteen-year-old Toumanova and
Baronova as stars. The fact that they had other merits
speedily dawned on the public. They attracted immediate
attention by their technique, they retained it through their
artistic instinct. It was too early to discuss conscious artistry.

De Basil banked everything upon the success of three
unknown children: Toumanova, Baronova,· and Riabouchinska. He was careful to give them the support of
experienced artists, but the onus of the performance fell
on them, Danilova only joining the company later, and with
them began the world-wide popularity of ballet. In
Diaghileff's day ballet as a whole rather than individual
dancers had attracted the attention; with de Basil it was
the opposite. The young dancers became stars, the public
went to see them, and remained to enjoy the art.

The new company made its début in Monte Carlo in
1932, and was a success. In Paris also the critics acclaimed it. But there was still a difficult time ahead,
during which de Basil fully proved his fine powers of
leadership. The company toured Holland, Belgium, Germany, and Switzerland, in a constant struggle to survive.
The expenses were heavy, the repertory small. During
those difficult times, when salaries were delayed and artists
hungry, not one member of the company deserted and the
ensemble was preserved. It required not only courage but
an unusual knowledge of human nature to keep the enterprise alive. De Basil received at attractive offer to come
to England in 1932, but declined, feeling that the repertoire
was not yet sufficient. When he opened at the Alhambra
on July 4th, 1933, he was in a desperate situation. Within
a week he was safe; the ballet boom had started in England. Shortly before, he had suffered his first loss, that of
Balanchine, who left with Toumanova. Massine came in
as choreographer and then as artistic adviser, and Baronova
in *Les Présages* danced her way to fame. She was just
over thirteen.

In December 1933 the young company made its American début, the first of a series of yearly visits from coast to coast, under the ægis of a great impresario, S. Hurok, who revived an interest in an art that was moribund, associated in the mind of the American public with presentation numbers in movie houses.

(II)

The partnership of de Basil and Massine, which has undergone so many vicissitudes in and out of legal hands, has been a fruitful one.

It should be sufficient in a survey of contemporary ballet to analyse the ballets and the artists and so to give a complete picture of the scene. Unfortunately, in any discussion of Russian Ballet this is not enough. There are a number of unpredictable and extraneous events that occur to alter the whole direction of the art. During Diaghileff's lifetime, so great was his prestige that he had little to fear from opposition. He was the actual " inventor of a recipe "—his own words—and not one of the many would-be heirs. In contemporary Russian Ballet politics, caused by the clash of personalities, is an all-important factor that the critic-historian cannot possibly ignore without giving an erroneous picture of the scene.

De Basil and his first collaborator, Réne Blum, soon found themselves in active disagreement. Blum had inherited Diaghileff's throne at Monte Carlo, de Basil his effective leadership of a troupe. Save during the seasons at Monte Carlo, Blum had lost active association with the company. Through this division the art received a serious set-back. René Blum,[1] a man of great culture in close contact with the leading artists of the day, could have contributed a great deal to the common cause. When the split came and the partnership was finally dissolved, de Basil lost Monte Carlo, and Monte Carlo is a trump card.

[1] René Blum has since died a hero's death in enemy hands.—A. L. H.

It has never been a great proposition commercially, but from the earliest years of the Diaghileff company, who attached the greatest value to it, it has been a centre for creation and recreation. The artists have time to rest and study, new ballets can be planned and then tried out on a sophisticated public, the scenery and costumes, worn through travel, can be renewed. To complete the loss René Blum started a new company, engaging Fokine to mount fresh works and supervise the production of his masterpieces. There may be a certain advantage in two large ambulant companies, so long as these are friendly. But if they play at the same time in the same city and compete for one another's artists, the public becomes confused and the art as a whole suffers.

The second serious split, between de Basil and Massine, took place in 1937. Whatever the definite cause, which cannot concern us here, there is always the general one of a lack of understanding between artist and manager. There is glory and to spare for each, but unfortunately at the time neither can realise it, and the result is conflict where there should be harmony.

Massine left de Basil to become the centre-piece of still another company, "The World of Art," that acquired René Blum's company and its works. With Massine went some of the most prominent de Basil artists, and de Basil changed his Prime Minister for the third time and secured Fokine as choreographer.

Now, it is obvious from this bald account alone that Russian Ballet cannot flourish artistically in such an atmosphere of change.[1] It takes many years to form an *ensemble* that can be destroyed in a few days. Also, the artists become so unsettled by intrigue that they are incapable of giving their undivided attention to the art. At the present moment the Russian Ballet is split into three

[1] Since this was written there have been so many changes that it is impossible for the historian to keep touch; but this more than proves my point.—A. L. H.

groups—the Ballet Theatre and the Monte Carlo Ballet in America, and de Basil's company at Buenos Aires in the Argentine. Many of the original dancers have deserted ballet for musical comedy and the films. One can only regret that " politics " have caused the disintegration of so remarkable an institution, and benefit by the example.

I have dealt with these ballet " politics " here, for a definite reason, before trying to assess the work done during the five years' boom. I believe that they are caused by the lack of a fixed creative policy fully as much as that they are the cause of it: the signs of an artistic degeneracy, though a very brilliant one. All the symptoms are present, even the unbalanced hysteria of an audience on the subject of individual performers that was also so prominent in the great decline following the romantic period.

In my chapter on Diaghileff I analysed the tendencies of the ballets produced at various periods and showed how the art had developed. The period of his greatest creative strength was when he produced that masterpiece of ballet, *Petrouchka*. The essence of his artistic leadership was discovery and harmony; the discovery of choreographers, musicians, and decorative artists, and the collaboration of these. The post-Diaghileff ballet has little to show in the way of discovery. It has developed dancing and choreography (but not fresh choreographers), neglected music and décor.

(III)

Its works fall under two headings: revivals and creations. It would be obvious to say that these revivals presented in a less perfect way works that had been done to perfection in the past; obvious and grossly unfair. There is always a type of mind ready to condemn the present in the name of the past: the type of mind that would have prevented Fokine in the name of Petipa and that so nearly succeeded that Fokine produced his masterpieces in exile. Even in the case of the most sincere, memory is flatteringly deceptive. Diaghileff understood this when he said that in order to revive *Scheherazade* it would be necessary to heighten all the colours, since memory would have made them seem many tones brighter. These revivals may have been given without the finish of former days, but the young artists have brought out other interesting qualities, and could we suddenly see the original productions we might easily find in them much that is stilted and old-fashioned. *Les Sylphides*—a manifestation of the romanticism that is ageless—is a great enough work to be interpreted by every generation, and every generation will stress some fresh aspect of its beauty. The very youth of its interpreters in 1933 was a quality. But in this same *Sylphides* one could see a lack of taste in production that is significant, the use of an enlarged painting by Corot as a backcloth. Benois' original décor still exists and could easily have been used. Such an idea could never have entered into Diaghileff's head. His work was planned as a whole. Today, the idea seems pleasant enough and without much deliberation it passed. Also the dancers have adopted a glamorous make-up from Hollywood, a little shocking in so fragile a work. There is insufficient time for thought when economics make hurry and constant travel a necessity. De Basil inherited much of the Diaghileff repertoire, and we must be grateful to him for making it live again as well as he has done. Criticism on that score is superficial.

It is in the new works that this brilliant degeneracy can be felt: the tendency to " get away with things." To start with, the new repertoire is, with one exception, by choreographers already famous before or immediately after the 1914 War. *Massine produced his first work in 1915, today he is still the biggest figure in contemporary ballet.* The new ballet has not yet produced its own choreographer capable of leading the young generation of dancers. Choreographers may be born and not made, but they must certainly find a congenial atmosphere in which to develop. I have discussed Diaghileff's strength as a pedagogue. No talent could escape him. Today, there is no one who can guide the budding choreographer; consequently there is no young choreography. In a decade this will be obvious. It is the major failure of post-Diaghileff ballet, a business living on its capital, which is fortunately immense and can tide it over a few more years.

The one exception is David Lichine. That he has natural ability he has abundantly proved, but there is a doubt whether that ability will ever be fully exploited. His first two works, *Nocturne* and *Les Imaginaires,* were failures, and clearly through no fault of his own. They were rushed on, their material was ill-digested, and Lichine was not surrounded, as Massine and Balanchine had been, by artists of experience ready to guide him in matters of taste and planning. His third ballet, *Le Pavillon,* to well-arranged music by Borodin, showed his best work to date. It was a true romantic ballet arranged with great skill especially in the handling of the *corps de ballet,* always a good sign. The beginner can often arrange an effective *solo* or *adagio* out of his own muscular feeling. His fourth ballet, *Francesca da Rimini,* has been his most spectacular. He succeeded in telling a dramatic story with great power, handling climax after climax until the final telling scene of Francesca's murder with a magnificent sense of the theatre. It was, indeed, grand theatre, if a trifle " ham," but not much else, and again through no fault of Lichine's. He was given the time and the opportunity to study in Italy, but the music was ill-chosen and contradicted all the sound-principles of ballet composition. Tchaikovsky's symphonic poem, *Francesca da Rimini,* whatever its merits as music, was written round an idea that is entirely different from the scenario given to Lichine, with the result that in whole passages music and action clash. Such a positive story demands music commissioned for the purpose. There is the exception of *Scheherazade,* but then the action was deliberately fitted to the music by such a skilled committee as Diaghileff, Fokine, Benois, and Bakst.

Lichine's next ballet, a revival of *The Gods Go a-Begging* to new choreography, was thrown on in a few weeks. It has its moments of charm, it was beautifully interpreted, but haste marred the climax, one of the weakest seen in ballet for a very long time. The whole work compared unfavourably with de Valois' version at Sadler's Wells, though the *solos* and the *adagio* were more effective. The English work was planned, the Russian just happened. Finally, in *Le Lion Amoureux*, the only opportunity Lichine was given to work to a commissioned score, that score was a handicap. It was impossible to fit to it a developed story, since in its manner and form it resembled the incidental music of a film. Once again it is important to stress the fact that neither Lichine nor the composer is to be blamed, but the system, or rather the lack of it. There should be a supervision that is both tactful and effective and that sees that score, story, and movement are suitably wedded. In his last production to be seen in England, *Protée*, he has produced a small work of great sensibility that justifies a strong belief in his future.

Lichine has had considerable success with the ballet *Graduation Ball*, shown in Australia in 1939. Lately he has been producing ballet for operette, musical comedy, and the films.

This sketch of the career of an exceptionally talented boy is revealing. By comparison with the other phases of ballet I have commented on, it shows that we have reached an unfortunate period of easy box-office success, difficult artistic success, and this may mark the end of the boom— the very word itself suggests a slump—instead of the beginning of something new which the youth of those concerned should announce.

(IV)

The greatest and most sensational successes of the new Ballet have been Massine's three symphonies. These works have aroused a fierce controversy that has helped to popularise them.

I will summarise the arguments pro and con without myself taking a determined stand on either side, or, perhaps, taking yet a third position; not that I have ever believed in sitting on the fence, but because the evidence here seems to warrant it.

The musical purists maintain, and rightly so, that a symphony is a complete and independent work of art; consequently that anything that is added to it is completely superfluous; that it does not lend itself either to amplification or to illustration. In 1909 the musical purists made the same objection against *Les Sylphides*, reinforced by the fact that Chopin's music had to be orchestrated. While *Les Sylphides* and *Carnaval* are the beginnings of using music for ballet written for another purpose, one must not drive the comparison too far. No one claims that their music is *absolute* in the same sense as the symphonies, and the choreographer has some powers of selection denied him in a continuous forty-five-minute composition. I merely mention this early objection to show that the musical purist tends to think in terms of the concert-hall rather than of theatrical effectiveness. The ballet is essentially theatre, and good theatre can under certain circumstances excuse what is bad taste on paper. The musical purist is invariably right on paper. The main question in the case of the symphonies is whether the circumstances excuse the use of this particular music.

The ballet die-hard, frequently more emotional than thoughtful, replies with a number of arguments. His main contention is that the choreographer does not seek either to amplify or illustrate this absolute music, but to create movement that is parallel in thought. Also, he goes on to say that any music that inspires a muscular reaction is suitable for dancing, and that this music very clearly does or it would not be danced to at all. He finally begs the purist to stay away and let him enjoy his ballet symphony in peace, even if there are grave doubts about its artistic taste.

My own reaction is somewhat between the two. I believe that the symphony by its nature is unsuited to ballet and that the almost complete success of three symphonic ballets proves nothing, especially since two of them are not typical, and the one that is is the weakest. The ballet symphony can never develop into a school. These particular ballets are isolated experiments in which Massine has succeeded to an astonishing degree in creating a parallelism of movement and sound and in so doing has extended the repertoire of choreography. It is in the more architectural grouping, beautiful in itself, that one finds the impossibility of any parallelism. The music does not allow the dancers to leave the groups that have been assumed, and the breakaway is clumsy and suddenly separates motion from music. This is especially noticeable in the first part of Berlioz' *Symphonie Fantastique*. Both *Les Présages* (Tchaikovsky's 5th Symphony) and Berlioz' *Symphonie Fantastique* lend themselves to a story; in the second part of the Berlioz Massine has devised some of the noblest choreography of our age; in the second part of the Tchaikovsky some of the most moving and theatrically effective. It is in the Brahms that the choice of music has been the least happy. For the first of many visits the plastically minded, as opposed to the musically minded, take in only the magnificent moving frescoes; it is with repeated visits that the difference between music and movement becomes noticeable and finally jars in such places as the *fouettés* and the *tours-en-l'air* of the final tableau. Such typical classroom virtuosity does not parallel the musical thought, which is lost when the music degenerates into a rhythmic accompaniment. These works are outstanding examples of great choreography, yet I would hesitate before calling them great ballets in the sense that *Petrouchka* is so unquestionably a great ballet. They lack that element of completeness. To use a colloquialism, "Massine has got away with it." Whether he or anyone else will do so again is another matter. The failure of the

Beethoven 7th Symphony, apart from the noble second movement, shows that. They would be ill-advised to try.

With the exception of *La Symphonie Fantastique,* with its attractive settings by Bérard, the symphonies have failed decoratively, and decoration is an essential in a work that aims at a parallelism of impressions from eye and ear. Masson's much-debated backcloth in *Les Présages* had a definite aim: to continue the movement of the dancers, and its surrealism was a success that a more positive picture could not have been. But the costumes of Fate and Frivolity were banal in the extreme. In *Choreartium* nothing could have been farther from the spirit of the music than the trivial décor and costumes. This same work rehearsed in practice costume was doubly effective.

(v)

Of the works to commissioned music *Jardin Public* was a failure, but to my mind not an entirely dishonourable one. Its failure was used to point out the merits and advantages of using well-established music. It did nothing of the kind, merely proving that one composer had failed in one score, and that particular composer a discovery of Diaghileff's. There was in this ballet at any rate a complete unity between music, story, and movement, and it failed as a whole, though much of the choreography deserved a better fate. *Union Pacific* was a success chiefly on account of the remarkable barman's dance that Massine had given himself, but it was also a far cleverer ballet than one might at first think. It was a genuine balletic translation of Americana, based on " folk-lore," a *tour de force* for a Russian choreographer, just as Nabokoff's clever cacophony was based on popular melodies. The failure of *Le Lion Amoureux* we have already discussed.

This is scarcely an inspiring record on the musical side for six years' work, and the fact that Russian Ballet has had six years of success speaks a great deal for the capital upon which it has been living. *The encouragement and discovery of composers and painters is Russian Ballet's immediate task.*

(VI)

In this brief analysis of the work accomplished during his reign we have left de Basil, the man, out of the account in a way that has been quite impossible in the case of Diaghileff. Diaghileff was a dictator; de Basil, a strong man, is a limited monarch, that is the great difference. But after the almost aggressive individualism of a Diaghileff, Russian Ballet needed de Basil, and owes him a debt of gratitude that is sometimes grudgingly withheld.

Where the ballet today suffers is through artistic starvation. Diaghileff once said during a Monte Carlo *première*: "Were the theatre to burn down tonight, every creative artistic talent in Europe would perish." He was right, his audience was a complete artistic Who's Who. All were his friends, members of his parliament, the majority there as his guests. Today, the ballet no longer has such friends, it is completely surrounded and almost stifled by business executives, and the artist is called in to do one definite job in a desperate hurry. We have seen the folly of that. Everyone in ballet is vitally interested in the other man's job. Economics may seem to demand this over-commercial attitude, but in the long run it is a singularly short-sighted policy, and policy is a wrong word to describe what actually is a case of muddling through. The Russian Ballet has inherited Diaghileff's works, but it is rather our own modest Sadler's Wells that has inherited his viewpoint; greatly helped by a permanent home, it is true.

The hope for Russian Ballet after a period of what can only be described as brilliant degeneracy lies in a speedy and complete union of the two conflicting groups—in artists, not lawyers—and in a programme that includes the creative painters and composers of the day: in less politics

117

and more art. The dancing is healthy, though the dancers are sadly overworked, but the ballet itself is weak. Now that de Basil has accomplished the gigantic task of popularising the art, it rests with him and his advisers and in equal measure with Massine, still the dominating figure creatively, to give us something fresh and constructive. To mark time any longer is dangerous. The new Russian Ballet is as rich in names as any previous company. Its members must go forward together in complete harmony or their place will surely be taken by the many healthy young national movements that have been born of the urgent necessity for self-expression, and through the glorious example given them by Russian Ballet.

(II) Ninette de Valois

Edris Stannus, an Irish dancer who assumed the name of a line of French kings, much to Diaghileff's disgust—he always insisted on spelling it Devalois—is the only personality with a double claim to belong to this section of our study. As an animator of the Diaghileff—de-Basil type, she has founded a truly national ballet that is important enough to be considered internationally; as a choreographer she is a pioneer in England, as well as one of the two major women choreographers in the history of the art. She has still a third claim, as a teacher who has discovered and launched an entire company.

She started in the worst manner possible, as a child prodigy at a time when child prodigies and English (Irish) dancers were by no means the fashion. It was still necessary to adopt a change of name. De Valois herself *a changé tout cela*. She even survived such enthusiastic criticism as "that charming child genius" and "the child is a poem," tributes I have preserved in my collection of curiosities. De Valois was an admirable dancer with a fine technique and an intelligence that informed all her work. But it is not as a dancer that she gains her outstanding position in the history of ballet.

After a variety of engagements she joined the Diaghileff company in 1924 as a small *soliste*, her finest work being the "finger variation" in *Aurora's Wedding*. She used her time there to study methods of teaching and production, a child among them taking notes; dancing was never an end in itself. Two years later she left the company, dissatisfied with the ballet æsthetic of the day. She founded a school of her own with what seemed at the time the pompous and ambitious title of the Academy of Choreographic Art. This she used as a headquarters, travelling to Dublin to produce for the Abbey Theatre and to Cambridge for the Festival Theatre. Her work in these theatres, in addition to her experience of pure ballet, decided her future bent. Working with actors unused to movement in the dancing sense, she was compelled to use theatrical production that would be effective. She gained at this time a rare conception of the relation between ballet and theatre. Fokine, a great producer quite apart from his choreography, was also trained in the dramatic schools. It is characteristic of de Valois that on the very first occasion that she met Robert Helpmann she said to him: "Something can be done with that face," thinking in a direction alien to the ordinary choreographer.

There seemed to be something a little smug and ridiculous about this young dancer who disapproved of the direction that the greatest of all companies was taking, and who formed her own Academy. It must have required an almost overpowering self-confidence. To have paused to examine the situation even for an instant would have meant failure. Thousands of dancers must have envied her the excellent position in the Russian Ballet, and she gave it up simply to follow a line of her own at a time when it was quite impossible for anyone but Diaghileff to gain a hearing. This stubborn determination against what seems at the time to be common sense is characteristic of Ninette de Valois.

The first works that she produced did not seem to justify

her decision, even when one made due allowance for the
material available. They showed the urgent desire to
express something strong, they were well produced, dull
because she was so obviously in earnest and almost ridicu-
lously young.

A critic who did not flair anything more than worthy
determination at the time of *Rout*, a naïve mixture of
Central Europe and Celtic Twilight, can scarcely blame
himself for a lack of perspicacity. There were violent extremes in de Valois' artistic conceptions, between brutal
masculine strength and finicky, fluttering, feminine weakness. The one quality that characterised her work was
musical conscientiousness, amounting at times to pedantry.
She has a knowledge of musical construction that is rare
in anyone.

Until the formation of the Camargo Society, 1930, she
had proved nothing positive. I would even say, from my
own observations and from the talk of dancers, that as a
producer she was then inclined to drill all the personality
out of her cast, counting the music till mathematics had
driven the atmosphere away.

The first revelations were the Camargo productions, *Job*
and *La Création du Monde*. Here were big conceptions
treated in the grand manner. One hesitated to call them
ballets, rather grudgingly even, but one began to look at
de Valois in a new light, to see that she was neither smug
nor cantankerous, but someone with a great deal to express
and the necessary craft with which to express it. A pretty
Cephalus and Procris and an intolerably dull *Origin of
Design* seemed to confirm the original impression that she
was not truly a choreographer. Their craft was competent,
but they never came to life, certainly they never even gave
a hint of the personality of their creator.

The Camargo Society undoubtedly had a marked effect
on Ninette de Valois apart from the opportunity it gave
her. It turned the earnest young rebel into someone who
could value and understand the full meaning of collabora-

tion. It brought her into contact with others who were trying to create, curbed some of her intolerance, turning it into a creative channel.

When Lilian Baylis summoned Ninette de Valois to work at the Old Vic, two women admirably calculated to understand one another met. Lilian Baylis had a one-track mind, the success of her theatre; de Valois also, the success of her ballet; and, since the tracks led in the same direction, the force was irresistible. The essence of Lilian Baylis's success was a knowledge of human nature and the bigness of character to put implicit faith in anyone in whom she had learned to believe. And she believed in de Valois enough to let the handful of girls composing the opera ballets grow into a permanent ballet company. Looked at in cold blood by someone who knows the full difficulties, both women seemed insane.

De Valois must undoubtedly have made a considerable sacrifice to undertake what seemed an incredibly uphill task. Her school was a commercial success and she was beginning to make a name. Unhesitatingly she threw all her resources into the new enterprise and closed the school, accompanied by her pupils and a charming dancer, Ursula Moreton, as assistant. The company in the beginning was merely an embellishment to the opera, and attracted very little attention. One had to be a blind patriot to talk of British Ballet. Lilian Baylis was willing to gamble on its success, de Valois was building deliberately and systematically. The Wells then engaged Alicia Markova (and, at times, Anton Dolin) as a guest artist. Markova had a very considerable public who learnt the way to Rosebery Avenue, and the help that she gave the young enterprise was invaluable, though artistically, at the time, the partnership did not show great results. Markova was the solitary star, the Wells company a background devoid of personality. The ballets were built round Markova, the classics were revived for her, and it was obviously impossible to give to any of the young dancers roles in which she was shining. In any case, they were not yet ready. The ease of her position, the lack of any cause for apprehension that it might be menaced, would not have benefited Markova in the long run. With considerable foresight she decided to leave. The general opinion was that her absence would kill the Sadler's Wells Ballet, and there were talks of engaging another *ballerina*. Wisely this was not done. It would have strangled the enterprise.

Then Ninette de Valois revealed herself, within a few weeks, not only as a choreographer—after *The Rake's Progress* we were beginning to realise her strength—but as an animator, organiser, teacher. The company suddenly came into being, from one week to another, almost dramatically. The outsider could have no perception of the intensive preparation that had been going on. The opportunity arose and the company was ready; young, a trifle raw, but a genuine personality, where before it had been a group of schoolgirls and boys. The seasons that followed this birth of the company—for the company was born the very moment it could rely on the dancers it had itself formed—proved a striking testimony to the leadership of de Valois. Progress was normal, that was the keynote of the work. If a dancer showed promise she developed gradually, not shining one week and a total eclipse the next. The erratic brilliance of the young Russians had made us forget the meaning of normal progress.

De Valois has discovered and developed an altogether extraordinary amount of talent. I do not believe that it is the result of flair, so much as knowledge. She has the ability to see what the result must be, if such and such a course of conduct is followed in the case of such and such a dancer. She is not misled by early success or failure; she has her own very positive ideas about talent that are frequently in open contradiction to those around her, and time and time again she has been right, right because she knows and not by intuition. She does not wait for the talent to declare itself, but waits for the right moment and then openly intervenes. The most extraordinary development has been the progress from the rather dry pedagogue to the truly creative teacher, a thing difficult to account for, unless the dry pedagogue never existed save in the minds of the onlookers. Yet pupils of pre-Wells days have confirmed it. Perhaps close contact with the fine musical mind of Constant Lambert has helped her to set in order her own musical knowledge and to see beyond the actual construction.

De Valois' knowledge as a teacher does not stop at a very thorough understanding of classicism, or of music. She has both a knowledge of anatomy and an eye for line that enable her to diagnose and treat the slightest anatomical abnormality, a gift which has enabled her to develop much talent that would otherwise have been irretrievably lost.

I have mentioned de Valois' understanding of classicism, without which it would be impossible to be the leader of an Academy. De Valois, the rebel, not only had no such understanding but obviously very little sympathy for pure classicism. It is interesting to speculate when such a change came about. It seems reasonable to ascribe it to the influence of having a close contact with such a dancer as Alicia Markova, for whom *Giselle, Casse-Noisette,* and the *Swan Lake* were revived. Previously to that, de Valois' classical knowledge must have been confined to the rather sterile atmosphere of the classroom, a sound knowledge of the mechanics, since she was a prominent pupil of Cecchetti, but without an opportunity for artistic perception. During her period with Diaghileff, shortly after the sensational failure of *The Sleeping Princess,* the classics only existed in the one-act abbreviation, *Aurora's Wedding,* and classicism was at a low ebb. When Sergueeff revived these great works from his system of notation, the producer in de Valois must have played a large part in bringing them to life.

I have said that de Valois, like all pioneers and leaders

of an artistic movement, has a one-track mind; it is also, in another sense, a large mind. The success of her own works is not her main preoccupation. She sees them almost impersonally, as one part of her main task. Never before in the history of repertory ballet have there been two resident choreographers working in close harmony. The case is still more difficult to conceive when one of them is a director of the company. De Valois has given to Frederick Ashton the most extraordinary support, whether she sees eye to eye with him or not. She has never denied to him the right of independent creation or even attempted to influence his productions. After a long experience of ballet, I marvel at the possibility of such a thing. That clear perception has meant that the Wells has been able to enlarge its scope in half the ordinary time.

De Valois is a thinker, a methodical worker in the great tradition of the *maîtres de ballet* of the past. She has outlined her ideas in a work of great value, *Invitation to the Dance*. It is vigorous, stimulating, and very revealing of her personality. The fighter and the rebel still exist alongside of the successful leader of an Academy. It is both intolerant and infinitely understanding. It shows an exuberant temperament that can curb itself only to self-discipline, and de Valois' whole progress has been the steady acquiring of that discipline. She has made her rebel's nature richly creative. She overworks the entire time, but her work is planned and productive.

She is today the outstanding figure in the world of ballet; her accomplishment as a leader greater than anyone else's and certainly less disputed.

Her musical knowledge, her ability to express herself on paper, her choreography, pedagogy, and direction of a theatre bring one back to the heroic days, stressing once again the crying need for a higher education in dancing.

The scheme for the Vic-Wells Ballet school, which aims at the creation of a veritable conservatoire of ballet and the arts that compose it, may meet this need, if it can find a Mæcenas. So many are willing to contribute large funds to present works of art, sometimes of doubtful attribution, to the nation; so many donate large sums for the excellent cause of providing playing-fields that there is surely hope. The Vic-Wells scheme aims at the creation of living works of art, works that can give constant employment to many, and that can provide mental recreation at a small cost to countless thousands to whom ballet will give solace. *Lilian Baylis created a theatre that is more truly national than any State institution, since it was born out of the sixpences of the masses.*

(III) MARIE RAMBERT

When the history of English Ballet, so recently born, comes to be written, the name of Marie Rambert will have an especially prominent position, for she it was who, pre-Camargo, pre-Wells, showed that the English girl had something to express as a dancer and was not merely fit for relegation to the back row of a Russian *corps de ballet*. It is not the Russians, by the way, who believed in the inferiority of the English girls, but the great British public itself. Sokolova, Markova, Dolin, proved nothing; they were magnificent freaks; besides, they were very heavily disguised, and not everybody knew the ghastly truth about their passports. Diaghileff himself believed in the English, marvelled at their aptitude, and said that one day they would have a ballet of their own.

Marie Rambert was the first to present a whole group of young *solistes* under their own, or at any rate, British, stage names. They were interesting, these youngsters, and their youth itself was an extraordinary novelty. We had yet to meet de Basil and his babies. Providence was kind to English Ballet, allowing it four years between the last Diaghileff Season, Covent Garden, 1929, and the first de Basil Season, Alhambra, 1933, in which to be born and grow strong enough to continue life.

Marie Rambert came comparatively late to ballet, having specialised in the Dalcroze movement, and it was as an expert teacher of eurhythmics that she made her first contact with Russian Ballet. Whatever influence she may have had over the Russians, they completely won her over to ballet and she became an ardent pupil of Cecchetti.

The fact that she started late and did not have much opportunity to practise her art has had an enormous bearing on her personality and has given her the burning desire to continue dancing vicariously. Marie Rambert is not a choreographer, and not a teacher in the ordinary sense of the word, but a frustrated dancer who makes others dance in her place. For this reason her influence has been genuinely creative.

After a season of public performances at which Karsavina consented to appear with her young prodigies, Marie Rambert started the Ballet Club, an old parish hall rebuilt and embellished by her husband, Ashley Dukes, into an elegant *bonbonnière* of a theatre. This was the first permanent home of ballet in England; a self-contained unit, a theatre with a company and a school of its own. There Frederick Ashton did his first important work, William Chappell discovered his gifts as a designer, Harold Turner danced *Le Spectre de la Rose* well enough for Karsavina to pick him as partner, and Pearl Argyle, Maude Lloyd, Prudence Hyman, Andrée Howard, Diana Gould, and others began to interest a limited but artistically influential public. The coming of the Russians did not kill it, though it removed some of the company, among them Vera Nelidova (née Betty Cuff) and Lisa Serova (née Elizabeth Ruxton), who have been increasingly successful. The Ballet Club was one of the mainstays of the Camargo Society; in fact, together with Ninette de Valois, it *was* the Society, each one having a share in the indispensable Markova, who danced everywhere in those days, appearing for five minutes in a cinema for a substantial sum, dancing *Swan Lake* for love. The public has a strange sense of values at times.

The size of the Ballet Club stage has had a marked effect on Marie Rambert's work. It has denied her the culmination of her effort and its development to full maturity; also it has robbed her of much credit that is her due. Its advantages, and they exist, I will talk of later. The time must come when the dancer and more especially the choreographer grows cramped, physically and mentally. He requires the inspiration of an orchestra, a large stage, a big company, large audiences. If he does not feel this, there is something seriously wrong in his development. In the old days the goal was the Russian Ballet; today, it is Sadler's Wells, and Marie Rambert has seen a number of her finest " discoveries " express themselves most fully as truly mature personalities at Sadler's Wells: Argyle, Ashton, Turner, Chappell. She has had the uphill work of years, without the reward of seeing it finally coming to flower on her own stage.

Marie Rambert has immense flair for talent, and a nervous, vital enthusiasm. It seems to me that her *forte* has been in developing the very young whom she can guide artistically, and that her personality may prove too powerful for the artist who has passed the apprenticeship stage; resulting either in a conflict or in the submission of the artist, a bad thing, even when he is wrong, and Marie Rambert is an acute analytical critic when her enthusiasm is held in check.

Where Marie Rambert has excelled is in seeing beyond the teaching of technique, in drawing out creative gifts. She is no choreographer, yet she taught Ashton, Anthony Tudor, Andrée Howard, Frank Staff and Walter Gore to be choreographers; she made Chappell design. She has shown that a dancing-school must be something more than a physical-training ground: it must be a cultural centre. Her gifts of intelligence, culture, and wit have been of inestimable service to her pupils.

The advantages of the small stage are that experiment becomes economically possible. No one with a large theatre and an orchestra to pay can afford to take any risks. Russian Ballet, today dependent on its own resources, has been relying for the most part on the choreographers developed by Diaghileff. Sadler's Wells is now too big a concern to risk a failure, but Marie Rambert can and must take risks. Temperamentally such a function suits her well, and she has the necessary flair to make it worth while. It is a significant fact, of which one might easily lose sight today, that from the first her experiments on that small stage were taken seriously by everyone and were never considered as pupil shows. She could have received no more genuine praise than that. Once the " discoveries " are assets they will leave her; they may not be grateful to her—" discoveries " so seldom are—but she will have had the satisfaction of the work itself.

Another field in which Marie Rambert has taken the lead is in the formation of a new branch of the art of ballet, the miniature or chamber ballet, and she has already sponsored some charming productions of that kind, the work of one of her original company, Andrée Howard, both designer and choreographer, who is able to make a virtue of the small stage and who, in *Death and the Maiden* and especially *Lady into Fox,* has created works of real skill and beauty.

Marie Rambert, more than anyone today, has set out with deliberation to find choreographic talent. She sees it latent in every pupil, she is boisterously optimistic, able to make others believe, including the would-be choreographer himself. And strangely enough, the talent often is there in sufficient quantity to reward her for her flair and courage.

(IV) FREDERICK ASHTON

Whenever a man accomplishes anything unusual, generally in the realm of crime, it is customary for the press to comment on the fact that he is a public-school boy. Frederick Ashton, after passing his youth in South

Seymour

IRINA BARONOVA
*The Queen of Shemakhan
in " Le Coq d'Or "*

Anthony

BERYL GREY *in* "*Swan Lake*"

Anthon

ROBERT HELPMANN *in* " *Comus* "

Iris

TATIANA RIABOUCHINSKA as *Frivolity* in " *Les Présages* "

Harlip

PEARL ARGYLE in " *Lac des Cygnes* "

Anthony

PAMELA MAY in " *The Prospect Before Us* "

Mandinian

ROBERT HELPMAN in *"Miracle in the Gorbals"*

Tunbridge-Sedgwick

MARGOT FONTEYN in "*Swan Lake*"

Anthony

BERYL GREY and DAVID PALTENGHI in "*Promenade*"

SALLY GILMOUR
in " Lady into Fox "

G. B. L. Wilson

ALEXANDRA DANILOVA and LEONIDE MASSINE in "*La Boutique Fantasque*"

Anthony

MARGOT FONTEYN *in* "*Le Spectre de la Rose*"

Anthony

NINETTE DE VALOIS

Anthony

MOYRA SHEARER *in* "*Promenade*"

Anthony

PAULINE CLAYDEN *in* "*Promenade*"

(Below) TAMARA TOUMANOVA *in* " *La Symphonie Fantastique* "
(Opposite) ALICIA MARKOVA *in* " *Swan Lake* "

Seymour
Brewster

Mandinia

MARGOT FONTEYN, ALEXIS RASSINE and GORDON HAMILTON in
" Carnaval "

America, was educated at a public school, a startling beginning to a successful career in ballet.

He started dancing by taking a lesson a week with Massine, and then joined Ida Rubinstein's company, coming under the influence of Nijinska. Those expensive ventures of Ida Rubinstein, eight months of rehearsal for a week of work, have proved of infinite importance in the history of contemporary ballet, giving us Lichine, Shabelevsky, Verchinina, Morosova, and others: a fact that should be placed to her credit.

Ashton must be considered a pupil of Marie Rambert, who gave him discipline, opportunity, guidance, and then a platform. He made his choreographic début in a revue at the Lyric, Hammersmith, with a small work, *The Tragedy of Fashion*. It was with the *Capriol Suite* and *Leda* that he showed marked ability. Pavlova greatly admired the former when it was shown by the Camargo Society, and came to a studio rehearsal of the latter. She was about to engage Ashton when she died so tragically.

It will be seen that Ashton enjoyed immediate recognition, and that his début was marked by an almost total lack of struggle. There was, however, a hard struggle to learn dancing at all, with an unhappy period in the city during which the precious time seemed to be slipping away. In this struggle Ashton revealed determination and character that were never missing even when he seemed to be enjoying a too great early success. He created each work with altogether extraordinary ease. The result was always highly effective theatrically, elegant, with an original angle, but somewhat derivative technically; first-class entertainment, but lacking in body. First for the Ballet Club, then for the Camargo Society, he produced a succession of works, many of which have survived, all of which met with success. His first large-scale production was *Pomona*. It launched the Camargo Society. It was definitely flippant, stylised Olympian, in a late Diaghileff vein, but it revealed the gift of being able to present his dancers to their very

greatest advantage. This he followed up with *Façade*
a still lighter work, but one that showed originality.

Ashton was from the first the very opposite of the othe
English choreographer, Ninette de Valois. She had a grea
deal to express and found difficulty in doing so; he ha
very little to say, but did so with extraordinary charm
She drew on her knowledge, he on his intuition. For
considerable period it looked as if he would go on eternall
showing promise, spoilt by his own gifts. Everything h
did was maddeningly charming and chic. Perhaps be
cause he was criticising himself at the time, he was bitterl
resentful of criticism.

In America he met with great success from a small cliqu
for his work in the Gertrude-Stein—Virgil-Thompso
Opera, *Four Saints in Three Acts*. This American ex
perience had a marked effect on his character. The en
thusiastic praise of a clique of æsthetes, couched in th
most extraordinary jargon, tickled his sense of humou
It was success of a type he no longer enjoyed. It gav
him an entirely new set of values.

There is also no doubt that for a very long time h
suffered from an inferiority complex, thinking of his ow
work in terms of the Russian Ballet and consequentl
rather despising popular success. This sense of inferiorit
completely vanished when he joined the flourishing Well
Ballet, and not only enjoyed the advantages of a permanen
company, but of the whole atmosphere of creation. I
gave him something in which he could believe, and als
threw him into close contact with Constant Lambert. In
stead of having to rely upon scraps of music hastily throw
together, he could now collaborate with a man who under
stood the relationship between ballet and music mor
clearly than anyone else. Where before intuition ha
made his success, he could now call on knowledge to hel
him out. He could express far deeper emotions becaus
he felt them. He had become a conscious artist. Man

[1] See page 164.

130

of his works were still light, *Les Rendezvous*,[1] for instance, but they formed a vivid contrast to what had gone before. For the first time he was really grappling with his material,

guiding it instead of making a surface effect. There was no need for strong external influences. He could listen to the music directly.

[1] See page 166.

In *Nocturne* he showed genuine compassion; in *Apparitions* a vivid imagination disciplined by strong musical suggestions; in *Le Baiser de la Fée* a still further musical comprehension, his choreography bearing the same relationship to orthodox classicism as Stravinsky's music did to Tchaikovsky, upon which it was based. In *Horoscope*,[1] for the first time he handled his *corps de ballet* with maximum effect, showing himself a master of choreography.

This gain of conscious artistry has in no way lessened the feeling of spontaneity that he has always shown and that is one of his greatest qualities. *The Wedding Bouquet* appears to be a light-hearted frolic; only with close study does one see that the effects are obtained legitimately, out of movement, and that the dancing itself is splendidly sound.

I have dealt with some of Ashton's later creations in another chapter.

[1] See page 168.

CHAPTER 6

Appreciation : Studies of Ballets in the Contemporary Repertoires

(A practical application of Chapter Three)

IN this chapter I am going to comment on a series of ballets that are in the regular repertoires of companies performing in England, studying them in the light of the background that forms the subject of the third chapter. I shall try to avoid the technique of the guide book that marks special beauties with one or more asterisks. I have no wish to foist my own taste too obviously on the reader; my aim is to give him sufficient data to form a considered opinion of his own, to counterbalance, perhaps, the often uncritical emotions aroused by watching a very favourite performer who can do no wrong.

I will deal with the history, the conception, the music, choreography, and drama. The personalities who composed them are already known to us.

(I) GISELLE

Romantic survival

Giselle, first presented in 1841, is the oldest ballet in the current repertoire, and has been given without interruption ever since its creation. Yet the history of its creation bears no hint that it was to be an enduring work.

Théophile Gautier, in reviewing Heine's *De l'Allemagne,* found himself fascinated by the legend of the *wilis*— maidens who have died before their wedding day and who come out of their graves at night in bridal dress to dance until dawn. Should any man be caught in the wood when the *wilis* are dancing, he is doomed to dance on and on until he drops dead from exhaustion.

From Heine's description of the legend, Gautier saw an

admirable theme for ballet, a romantic theme of beautiful women, white gauze, and German moonlight. Together with an experienced opera librettist, V. de Saint-Georges, he turned the theme into a story. The music by Adolphe Adam was written within a week, and the choreography devised as rapidly.

If we ask ourselves why this particular ballet has survived out of the countless works that enjoyed success, we shall not only be able to assess its particular value, but to learn something of ballet in general. The music does not account for the survival, though it is in every respect superior to the ballet music of its period. The most that one can say is that it has not prevented survival. It has today all the quaint charm of the romantic colour-print that one picks up for a few centimes on the Paris quayside. The ballet as a whole also has its quaint moments, but it is very much more than a museum piece. It is a moving, living work. *Giselle* survives because it is the purest expression of its period and because its story makes it the greatest of all tests for the *ballerina*. Every actress has the ambition at some time in her career to undertake the role of Marguerite Gautier in *La Dame aux Camélias*; every *ballerina* sees herself as *Giselle*. The parallel is exact in every particular. The old play is quaint, its mechanism is obvious, but it lives because it is magnificent theatre, and the chance it gives to the actress now delights Garbo or Yvonne Printemps as it did Sarah Bernhardt or Duse. The dancer in *Giselle* must have a very strong technical equipment, and in addition to that a great range of expression. She starts as a carefree village girl, fond of dancing and very much in love. Next we see her betrayed and driven mad, until she dies a suicide. Then, in the following act, she is a spirit who must impress upon us the fact that she is lightness itself and so make a vivid contrast with the red-cheeked villager of the first act. This acting raises innumerable difficulties. The scene of madness cannot be naturalistic or it would be altogether out of

Giselle.

the picture. It must be lyrical and fit perfectly within the classical convention. The latitude allowed the actress is minute, every gesture is circumscribed. To succeed in *Giselle* means a triumph of personality, a unique example of true personality that is technically disciplined.

Another reason for its survival lies in the fact that it is more perfectly balanced than the other romantic ballets. The male role exists in fact, and is not merely inserted for purely technical reasons. Nijinsky made a name in this ballet, Lifar and Helpmann have both proved the dramatic possibilities of the part. *Giselle* is not merely an excuse for dancing, but lives on account of the drama that it expresses. Of all the romantic ballets, one can rely only upon contemporary accounts; it stands alone in fulfilling the conditions laid down by Noverre.

Within living memory Pavlova was supreme in the role. To have seen her in nothing else is to have seen every facet of her art. She made one innovation to increase the plausibility of the scene, dancing the second act in draperies suggestive of grave clothes, instead of in the conventional ballet skirt. Unfortunately, after her the innovation has been abandoned. It is both logical and in a tradition that is older and more acceptable than that of the middle nineteenth century. After Pavlova only certain aspects of the complex role have been revealed. Olga Spessivtseva (Spessiva) has danced it with magnificent purity of line; Markova, for whom it was revived in England, gave an excellent academic rendering, especially of the second act; Margot Fonteyn, its latest interpreter, has stressed the tenderness of the character and more nearly resembles Pavlova than any other dancer I have seen in making one forget the mechanics of the *ballerina*.

To dance *Giselle* with any degree of success is to be a considerable dancer and an artist as well. The conception of the role rises above the quaint appealing music and the conventionally effective setting. The ballet lives because its central figure is a genuine character whose suffering can move one to compassion. The poetic inspiration of Heine and Gautier has shone through what has become a dead formula.

(II) THE SWAN LAKE: AURORA'S WEDDING
Classical survivals

The Swan Lake was first produced in 1877. It was of considerable importance and well ahead of its time in conception, since it meant that once again the serious composer was to be concerned in the making of ballet. Admirable though it is choreographically, its survival is certainly due to the music of Tchaikovsky. The only works of the period to survive are those by Tchaikovsky: *The Swan Lake, Casse-Noisette,* and *The Sleeping Princess*. At the time, his music was considered too symphonic in form to be suitable for the theatre. That alone reveals to us the true state of ballet and *balletomanes*.

The original production was a failure, and it was only after the composer's death that the work succeeded, when it was revived in 1894, with fresh choreography by Petipa, thanks to the enlightened rule of I. A. Vsevolojsky, director of the Imperial Theatres.

The Swan Lake presents an enormous contrast to *Giselle*. It is not so essentially romantic, though its music is truly romantic in contrast to the tuneful tinkle of *Giselle*. It has a story of the conventional romantic type with a heroine of dual personality who has been bewitched by an evil spirit. The story, however, is of no account. It is told, like *Giselle*, by means of conventional miming, but whereas in *Giselle* the actress-dancer can convey a depth of meaning outside the mime, in *The Swan Lake* the mime remains as a rather tedious interruption of the dancing; so much so that in many versions it has been heavily curtailed, and with no loss. The essence of *The Swan Lake* is its dancing, and the role was created for the greatest virtuoso of her day, Pierrina Legnani. It was her *fouettés* that caused a sensation, and not her acting.

Today, *The Swan Lake* in its entirety survives in Russia, the home of old-fashioned ballet, and at Sadler's Wells. The version that is best known is that used by Diaghileff,

a concentrated affair in one act. This, while it makes the ballet more acceptable to modern ideas, slightly distorts it, and the tendency has been more and more to attack it in the spirit of *Les Sylphides*, giving it a softness alien to

Petipa and his period. This one-act abbreviation dispenses entirely with one aspect of the heroine's dual nature, the hard facet in which she dazzles the Prince by her virtuosity. It dispenses also with the conventional act of *divertissements,* where a ball or celebration is used as an excuse to introduce various dances for their own sake, intruding on the narrative. The essence of the classical ballet is a very positive narrative that is disregarded in favour of showing as many aspects of dancing as possible. Ballet classicism departs a long way from the great masters who founded the art, and is to that extent misnamed.

In *Aurora's Wedding,* the other Petipa-Tchaikovsky survival, all that remains is the series of disconnected dances. In this respect it reveals the classical principle much more clearly than *The Swan Lake.* Diaghileff took the celebration scene from the full-length *The Sleeping Princess,* and added to it many dances from *Casse-Noisette.* That alone shows us the looseness of classical construction; dance for the sake of dancing, any excuse is justified so long as the dance itself is harmonious. Princess Aurora herself has no existence as a character. At her own wedding she is merely the *ballerina assoluta.* The second most important personages in the ballet, the Blue Bird and the Princess, appear only in the last act. Their dance is one of the gems of ballet, but if it were cut out entirely, it would not in any way alter the story of *The Sleeping Princess.* Also, even considered as a dramatic entity, the dance of the Blue Bird has no significance. Fokine's Dying Swan is a drama, Petipa's Blue Bird and Princess are brilliant dancers. Like a large canvas by Ingres, master of the French classical school of painting, this dance charms us by its line, delights us through its composition, but leaves us emotionally cold.

It must not be imagined on this account that these dances call for nothing but an accomplished technique. They also make considerable demands on artistry and personality. Nothing can more easily be rendered vulgar than

the Blue Bird or the Aurora *pas de deux,* if the dancer
concentrates on the steps at the expense of the dance as a
whole. Apart from technical ability, the quality to be
looked for in these classical dances is an interpretation that
removes them from acrobatics,[1] that gives them dignity
and purity. If the ballet has no entity of plot or structure,
each dance apart has a structural entity, and the great
classical dancer is the one who realises that conception.

(III) LES SYLPHIDES : LE SPECTRE DE LA ROSE

(I) *The new romanticism*

Les Sylphides, the best known and the most constantly
danced of all ballets, is an expression of the reaction in
Fokine against the artificialities of classicism. It does not
react against classical technique but against the parapher-
nalia that surround it. It is a return to romanticism, to
the true spirit of romanticism and not to its period expression. The period expression of romanticism dates; its
works, with the exception of *Giselle,* are dead; but the
romantic spirit itself survives at every period and in every
art.

Les Sylphides as first conceived by Fokine had a
standard romantic setting, the coming to life of images in
the mind of the fevered composer. Later, in 1908, it became the suite of dances that we know today, and Diaghileff
altered its original title of *Chopiniana* to that of *Les
Sylphides* for its presentation during his first Western
European season, Paris, 1909.

The title, suggested by Taglioni's famous ballet *La
Sylphide,* is particularly apt, for in *Les Sylphides* is preserved all that was best in *le ballet blanc.* Though the
work is composed of various disconnected dances (Chopin
Nocturne, opus 32, No. 2; *Valse,* opus 70, No.1; *Mazurka,*
opus 33, No. 3; *Mazurka,* opus 67, No. 3; *Prelude,* opus
28, No. 7, also used as the overture; *Valse,* opus 64,

---

[1] See page 41.

Les Sylphides

No. 2; and *Valse,* opus 18, No. 1), it is not a *divertissement.*
It has an absolute unity of atmosphere. The use of the
corps de ballet, making them into expressive artists instead
of a mechanical background, not only connects the whole,
but distinguishes the new romantic ballet from the classical and romantic works of the past.

The Swan Lake calls in the first place for the interpretation of a dance; *Les Sylphides* demands more; it demands
the interpretation of music. Though it has no direct
dramatic narrative, through this work the ghost of Noverre
is at last appeased. Logic enters once more into ballet;
music, atmosphere; movement, and costume are glori-
ously reunited.

(II) *Le Spectre de la Rose*

In this small work the shade of Théophile Gautier re-
visits the scene of his triumphs, and with it he enjoys a
posthumous success. So perfectly conceived is it, so
delicate, making such demands on its interpreters, that
today, though constantly given, it scarcely exists. It demands a dancer of exceptional virtuosity who will subor-
dinate himself to the role. The leap out of the window
that the audience have concentrated upon and will insen-
sitively applaud has killed the ballet. Fokine invoked
romanticism, the audience has insisted upon classicism,
and has been satisfied.

This ballet to Weber's *Invitation à la Valse,* directly inspired by a poem of Gautier's, tells the story of a young
girl returning from her first ball. She drowses, and the
spirit of the red rose that she has been given comes to
life and dances with her and then disappears. It is an
experience that happens but once in a lifetime. She
awakes disillusioned. The maiden has become a woman.
This ballet, properly understood, is the most perfect
theatrical expression of adolescence. Its misunderstanding
is due to the fact that while dramatically the leading role is
the woman's, from the dancing point of view the lead is

the man's. Today, neither dancers nor audience realise that fact. The man, the spectre of the rose, is dramatically on the second plane, a projection of the woman's dream. Only if this is made clear by the dancers does the ballet survive. The force of the woman's acting must eclipse the brilliance of the man's dancing, and the role is an exceptionally quiet one that calls for no obvious acting, but that must carry with it both conviction and sincerity. However brilliantly Nijinsky danced, the triumph was Karsavina's and she succeeded in recapturing it on every occasion, even when she danced with admittedly inferior partners. In difficulty the role is equalled only by that of *Giselle*. It calls for less sustained effort and for less technique, but for a far more subtle understanding of dramatic values. Since Karsavina, no dancer has deliberately succeeded; many *ballerinas* have made of it a dismal failure. The more accomplished the dancer, the worse the failure. Only certain immature dancers have instinctively captured something of the mood. If the audience would show more understanding and not applaud the leap in the middle of the girl's sad awakening, the ballet would have a greater chance of survival.

(IV) CARNAVAL

Porcelain mischief; another aspect of the new romanticism

Fokine's *Carnaval* to Schumann's music of the same name was composed hastily in 1910 for a charity entertainment, and was taken into the Diaghileff repertoire the following year.

It is slight, subtle, witty, tender, and pathetic; a quickly changing pattern of moods. Every dancer must be the interpreter of a carefully conceived role, in which period style plays its part. Delicate as porcelain, today it has " come to pieces in me 'and," and though it has been stuck together again, the rivets are painfully obvious. Ballet of this type can be preserved only when there is leisure to educate the dancers. For that reason the version given at Sadler's Wells, though far from satisfactory, since it has not had the advantages of direct contact with Fokine, is the most consistent to be seen today. The interpretation of *Carnaval* calls for infinite attention to detail. The fault of most productions is that the roles tend to become blurred and assume one another's characteristics. It would be difficult to imagine anything farther from dancing for the sake of dancing. Every little movement is an expression of character: Pierrot, lumbering and dejected, sentimental and credulous; Columbine and Harlequin playing the same game at the expense of the other characters, carefree and heartless, exploiting their brilliance and charm; Chiarina, also a flirt, more sentimental, deceiving herself at times; Pantalon, vain and pompous, the clubman " 'pon my word "; Papillon, flitting brilliantly through to mock at Pierrot. Today, the Philistines who intrude upon the scene, and make themselves the butt of all the characters, have very little meaning. We know " highbrows " and " lowbrows," but both are drab, both sneer at the romantic, and would be the butt of Fokine's enchanted and enchanting characters. Biedermeyer Germany is dead for ever—William killed it before Hitler—and *Carnaval* is as much the essence of Biedermeyer as *Giselle* is the essence of the more robust romanticism of its period. Bakst's delicate setting is an indispensable part of the ballet. Two attempts to use a new setting totally destroyed the work. The very fact that they should have been attempted showed a lack of understanding. *Carnaval* can only be understood by dancers and audience if it is seen as the definite expression of a period. Perhaps it will never really come to life again.

(V) SCHEHERAZADE: THAMAR

Exotics

Romanticism has always been interested in the exotic, and such ballets as *Revolt in the Harem* enjoyed a tremendous popularity. The new romanticism also turned to the exotic, and the flaming macaw-wing colours of Léon Bakst revolutionised decorative art.

There is nothing more dangerous dramatically than the exotic, which all too easily becomes ludicrous, like the Oriental department of a large emporium, and loses the essential plausibility. I have already discussed the genesis of *Scheherazade*. To many it will seem slightly old-fashioned, in the sense that it does not create the over-whelming impression it once did; but no one can find it comical, as they did *Cleopatra* when it was revived. The orgy is convincing. Cecil de Mille has yet to equal it, in spite of the lavish nature of his entertainments.

Scheherazade is brilliantly constructed round Rimsky-Korsakov's symphonic poem. Its blood-curdling narrative is well told, its characters wonderfully indicated. We know the imperious, sensual, vicious Zobeide, the kindly, weak, credulous Shah, his sceptical brother, as well as if they had spoken three acts of dialogue. They are " round " characters. How expressive the movement of the Shah's brother in kicking the body of the dead slave, as if to say, " You are about to forgive her and she gave herself to this." How telling the final scene between Zobeide and the Shah, an admirable example of what can be narrated through mime when it is handled by a master. The eunuch alone is " flat," a conventional comedy figure. He only accentuates the reality of the others. Finally, there is the study of the slave himself, the completely physical man, whom only ballet could exploit to the full. But characterisation alone would make this into a panto-mime. It has far more than narrative value. There is a richness of design that is interesting and logical in itself, movement that is exciting in itself apart from what it tells us. The slave's leap on to the cushion is an exciting athletic feat, as well as a demonstration of character. And Bakst's colours are a part of the music and the story. It is impossible to remove any element from this ballet without causing the collapse of the whole. The type of romanticism of *Scheherazade* is far removed from us to-day, but *Scheherazade* remains completely convincing, a vivid lesson in ballet composition.

Cleopatra has failed to survive. Its story is worth that of *Scheherazade,* some of its dances are exceedingly powerful, and Bakst's décor and costumes are good. It has failed because the music is a weak collection of hackneyed tunes, carrying no conviction. What should be pathetic has become comical, and we await in vain the entrance of Nervo and Knox to complete the fun.

Thamar, exotic sequel to *Scheherazade,* still survives. Balakirev's music is superior to Rimsky-Korsakov's, but not as ballet music. It lacks the directness. It tells the story in its own way, more completely. It is contemplative music rather than action music. *Thamar* is the study of one woman, and it lives only if that woman is a consummate actress. Its dances are, in a sense, a very conventional stage version of Caucasian folk-dances. There are none of the rich creations of *Scheherazade*. *Thamar* is never ridiculous, but it is only just alive.

(VI) The Polovtsian Dances from Prince Igor

The restoration of the male dancer

This ballet, the Polovtsian Dances from Borodin's opera, *Prince Igor,* more than anything secured the triumph of Diaghileff's Russian Ballet in Western Europe. An analysis of the first Paris press, 1909, clearly shows that the focal point was this essentially virile ballet.

When the Russian Ballet first came to Paris, its triumph was by no means assured. Ballet still survived at the Opéra, and Paris had seen many brilliant *ballerinas*. The male dancer no longer existed as an artist. The romantic credo and the outstanding success of Taglioni had reduced him to a secondary role. Romanticism in Russia had never gone to such extremes. Through the serfs, ballet had kept touch with reality. Ballet was not the plaything of poets. It had a solid contact with the people. Of the two brothers Petipa, Lucien remained in France and earned praise because he never obtruded himself, Marius went to Russia and became the Tsar of ballet.

Ballet, as we have shown, has as one of its ingredients *the orchestration of dancing*. Without the male dancer that orchestration is impossible. Male movement is the complement of female movement. When an all-male ballet performed in London it defeated its own object: it did not reveal male movement. Without any contrast the result was meaningless and monotonous. The weaker males were almost forced into the position of female impersonators. The result is equally bad in an all-woman ballet. Not only is the physical balance upset, but the dramatic as well, even when there is no concrete narrative. The *pas de deux* is more than a physical contrast: it is a love duet. There is this feeling of courtship in every *adagio*, even if it is as coldly classical as in *The Blue Bird* or as sublimated as in *Les Sylphides*.

For this very reason it may be taken as axiomatic that *the effeminate male dancer is a bad dancer*. There are altogether too many effeminate dancers in ballet. Effeminacy has became a bad tradition during the last twenty years, and is today causing untold damage, turning the virile athletic boy away from an art in which he could excel. Perhaps because dancing and the spirit of the old school tie, " play the game, you cads," seem so far removed, English male dancers are particularly effeminate, a very serious danger. Ballet originated with men, and is in no way incompatible with virility. Grace must not be confused with effeminacy: Carpentier was one of the most graceful creatures I have ever seen.

Prince Igor suddenly convinced Western Europe of the existence of the male dancer. His position in character ballet was immediately clear, but a misunderstanding still

147

persists as to his role in classical or romantic ballet. A romantic costume does not make a man effeminate. The most swashbuckling males wore what we would now term romantic costumes. Whatever his costume, the role of the male in ballet is that of a lover, and his physical attributes must be those of the star athlete. An understanding of this is essential. Without it ballet is in grave danger.

(VII) PETROUCHKA

The perfect dance drama

I have already written at some length of the origin of *Petrouchka*. It is indeed difficult not to quote it at all times as the perfect expression of the dance drama, rich in theme and colour, in character and pattern. It is the most truly Russian of all Russian ballets, its music and dancing inspired by the soil.

Its construction is interesting: a background of walkers-on who move and act but do not dance and who exist as individuals; next, the nurses, the coachmen, and the other characters who are also a part of the crowd, but who perform set national dances; and in the foreground the actors in the drama: Petrouchka, the Moor, the *Ballerina*, and the Charlatan. The audience is introduced to the characters first through the eyes of the spectators, then it is privileged to witness the drama as it develops behind the curtains of the booth, then once again it forms a part of the crowd to see the resulting murder, straying behind to watch the final triumph of Petrouchka. In this way the story is told from two angles and in complete detail. The whole thing is so simple that there is no need to refer to the programme for guidance, yet much more is expressed in the action than could ever be expressed in words. The characters are vividly contrasted: the Dancer, a heartless coquette; the Moor, a savage, strong and very physical, terrified of the unknown; Petrouchka, striving to express himself, in love with beauty, sawdust finding a soul. The

jostling, merry crowd of the first scene only accentuates the claustrophobia of poor Petrouchka in the second scene: one of the most pathetic to be seen on the stage. Although there are a number of seemingly independent dances, not one is there merely as an embellishment. They are all necessary to situate and to underline the tragedy. *Petrouchka* is told with extraordinary economy. *Le Coq d'Or*, equally Russian in theme, is verbose in parts, much of it is frankly spectacles. *The Firebird* is a fairy-tale far more poetically expressed, in every way a superior work, but *Petrouchka* stands alone. It is the *Hamlet* of ballet.

(VIII) L'EPREUVE D'AMOUR

A reminder

L'Epreuve d'Amour, or *Chung Yang and the Mandarin*, was produced by Fokine in 1936. I quote from the theatre programme: " When Leopold II came to the throne in 1790, a great change took place in the music favoured by the Vienna Court, and therefore in Mozart's professional duties. In the early months of 1791 he had to provide over forty dances—Minuets and so on—for the Court balls. For the carnival he provided an entertainment of the pseudo-Chinese type in vogue, for which he composed original music. This was subsequently lost, and has only recently come to light at Graz."

In its modern history a ballet using the original score was devised for René Blum by Fokine and Derain, who did the décors.

This simple work was misunderstood by many, chiefly among *balletomanes*, who were deceived by its simplicity and directness into thinking it childish, and who dismissed it as such. Had they examined it more deeply, they would have found in it a valuable lesson and a sharp reminder of the path that ballet must take, a reminder from the father of modern ballet. Since he left Diaghileff, Fokine has done no work more perfect.

L'Epreuve d'Amour

AMBROSE

The story is simple and easily rendered in pantomime. A mandarin's daughter loves a poor man. The mandarin is ambitious, and when a foreign ambassador comes, bearing lavish gifts, decides to give his daughter to him. The poor lover disguises himself as a dragon and terrifies the foreigner, while his friends, disguised as robbers, bind him and his attendants and remove the jewels. The mandarin, seeing that the foreigner has no more wealth, refuses the hand of his daughter. The treasure is then returned, but it is too late, and the mandarin is compelled to let his daughter marry the poor suitor.

The ballet opens and closes on a charming note, the mandarin in contemplation disturbed by the gambols of monkeys and the fluttering of a butterfly.

The style of the work is perfect. Fokine has not intended to depict China, but a *chinoiserie,* China seen through Occidental eyes, a fashion much in vogue in rococo times, as evidenced in porcelain, furniture, and wall decoration. He has set out to tell the simple story with directness of narrative and a characterisation that is a model of clarity, that is implicit in the particular piece of music, and that is not conventional.

One reaction, a false one, was to say: " This is not the best Mozart." Whether this is true or not is quite beside the point. We are not judging the music by concert-hall standards. It serves its purpose admirably, and reveals better than anything else the inadequacy of much considerably better music used unsuitably. The collaboration between Derain and Fokine is such as we have rarely seen in recent times, and Derain's colour scheme, daring and yet harmonious, is great theatre and great decoration.

This ballet is not academic, but it is a school piece in the best sense of the word.

. . . . . .

These Fokine ballets are the standard works of the repertoire. It is necessary to know them thoroughly before understanding ballet. A proportion of them must have been studied by every serious dancer, and those who have not interpreted their leading roles cannot be called *ballerinas*. The fact that, with the exception of *L'Épreuve d'Amour,* they were composed before the first World War does not mean that ballet has produced nothing since. What it does mean is that the dancer of today and the public of today have been brought up on them, that their continued and uninterrupted popularity testifies to their merit, and that they are performed by more than one company. They satisfy certain essential conditions so that, no matter how ballet develops, they will not lose their interest. Survival is an infallible proof of merit. Nothing could appear more old-fashioned today than certain of the ballets of the last Diaghileff period. They were amusing novelties, but bad works of art. The really fine work, unless lost by accident, expresses a constant truth.

I am going to comment on some of the more recent ballets that have points of special interest and that are to be seen almost every year.

The next group of ballets—they can also be called standard works—are selected from the great number created by Massine.

(IX) THE THREE-CORNERED HAT

And the " translation " of raw material

Spain, one of the few countries open to the Russian Ballet during the 1914 War, had a marked influence on Massine, since most of his formative period had been passed there. He had from the first produced various small works in the Spanish manner. Diaghileff had long been an admirer of Spanish dancing, and was in close touch with Picasso and Manuel de Falla. The result of all this was inevitably a Spanish ballet. Massine learnt the technique of the dance from a Seville gipsy, Felix by name. It has been said that this Felix, who subsequently went insane, was ill-used and actually composed the ballet. To anyone who has followed the argument of this book such a supposition is clearly absurd. Felix supplied the basic material, but he could be no partner to a Picasso or a da Falla. *The Three-cornered Hat* is a highly sophisticated work, a translation of Spanish folk-dancing into terms of the theatre. It could have been created only by an experienced choreographer. Massine used Felix's material, just as in other ballets he used the material of ballet classicism or of the museum.

This question of "translation" is all-important. Picasso did not copy traditional Spanish costume, he "translated" it for the stage; da Falla "translated" folk-music. The groundwork of *Petrouchka* is likewise a "translation" of Russian folk art. It could not have been created by a dancing coachman. Diaghileff, who more than anyone possessed both the instinct and the understanding of the theatre, always maintained that nothing is less convincing than the real thing brought on to the stage. A case in point was the ballet *Children's Tales*. A real horse brought on to the stage where everything else was stylised looked fantastic and out of place. It was necessary to "translate" the horse and to substitute a wooden one, which immediately fitted into the scheme. I have myself never seen anything more ridiculous than an elephant introduced on to the stage in an American picture-house version of *Scheherazade*. It made everything else look unreal. There are a number of Spanish dancers of exceptional virtuosity and artistry to whom the farucca in *The Three-cornered Hat* would be child's-play, but they could never make the impression of the Russian ballet dancer Massine. They might not even appear so Spanish. Their artistry is spontaneous and intuitive, his entirely conscious.

The failure of *Gaieté Parisienne* is due to a lack of this very "translation" in which Massine usually excels.

Appreciation

(X) La Boutique Fantasque

And the creation of character

La Boutique Fantasque, first presented in 1919, was planned in Italy during the War. Diaghileff decided to make a ballet out of certain pieces that Rossini had composed in his old age for the amusement of his guests. André Derain was chosen for the décor and costumes, and immediately proved himself a theatrical designer of the front rank.

The subject of toys coming to life at night is an old and obvious one for ballet. Pavlova had long made *The Fairy Doll* popular, but the music was too poor and the choreography too mechanical for it to have any existence as a work of art without her.

Massine brought an entirely fresh point of view to his choreography. He gave his toys character, avoiding the pitfalls of purely mechanical movement. From the very moment that we see them first of all as toys in the shop they have in them the possibility of independent life. The thing is so plausible that when it happens we are both charmed and convinced. The old shopkeeper is at first glance a ballet-type comic, but when he develops in his by-play with the young assistant, a typical Italian street urchin, we soon realise that he is a personality. The same with the Englishman and the Russian and their families. Observe how the Russian father counts and pays out the money. Even the maiden aunt is drawn in full. This ballet lives because it tells a familiar story in an unfamiliar way. We can make a not too far-fetched comparison with a novel by Dickens, a familiar theme enriched by the creation of a whole gallery of characters in the middle of which there is a delightfully sentimental episode.

The richness of the choreography is astonishing. Massine has "translated" movement from Italy, Russia, France, from the streets, from toys and paintings. There is never a moment of monotony, and music and décor are of a piece. The famous can-can requires a pure classical dancer to interpret it and once again reveals the infinite variety of ends to which the classical system is a means.

(XI) LE BEAU DANUBE [1]

Massine's tour de force

This ballet was devised by Massine immediately after his choreography for *Le Sacre du Printemps,* a complex work of incredible difficulty. It came to him easily, almost as a necessity, and at a time when jazz and not the Viennese waltz was the order of the day.

It seems obvious to construct a ballet round the melodies of Johann Strauss. It is so obvious that many have tried it, and failed. This music is almost a too complete expression of the dance itself. In *La Boutique Fantasque* the theme was obvious; here the music is, and once again Massine has accomplished a *tour de force* by creating a whole gallery of living people, and so telling a sentimental anecdote with remarkable style.

These characters are human and lovable. There is an interesting contrast between the two women who love the hussar: the timid young girl and the bold street dancer. The street dancer is vulgar, but once again the role calls for a pure classical dancer. The vulgarity must be balletic, never actual. One of the most remarkably conceived roles is Massine's own hussar. It is wrong to conceive of a ballet in terms of an individual dancer. I must be allowed to make of this case an exception. There is a moment in the story when the hussar stands in the centre of the stage motionless, reflecting while the other characters dance round and mock at him. That lack of motion must be positive; with nearly every dancer lack of motion is a negative. Massine and Helpmann almost alone possess this particular quality. When Massine stands there on the

[1] This refers to the original version before crude decoration ruined the balance of the work.—A. L. H.

stage he becomes the focal point; when any other dancer ceases to move he vanishes from our attention. Massine reveals this quality in two other roles. In *Le Chapeau Tricorne*, when the miller's wife is dancing and he is a spectator, he shows such positive concentration that he enhances her dance by making the actual audience concentrate. In *La Symphonie Fantastique*, when he is watching the pastoral movement one can feel that it is a part of his own life. These are the great moments of ballet, so subtle that they cannot be rewarded by applause; but they distinguish the true artist from the competent dancer.

Le Beau Danube is a fine enough ballet to make its effect without Massine, but without him it loses in meaning and intensity.

(XII) JEUX D'ENFANTS

And the decadent school

This was the first ballet that Massine arranged for the de Basil company, working with a group of young and inexperienced artists, whose technique was amazing and whose enthusiasm was infectious. It is admirably designed to exploit their particular gifts.

Jeux d'Enfants tells very much the same story as *La Boutique Fantasque*: the coming to life of toys, but in an entirely different manner. There is no attempt at any realism. He starts from an absolutely fresh viewpoint. All the happenings on the stage are fantastic. This needs explanation, for the word fantastic is a part of the title, *La Boutique Fantasque*. There the human characters are " real " and the toys are " real " until they come to life, and even when they come to life they are recognisable as toys; the fantasy lies in the fact of their coming to life. In *Jeux d'Enfants* the little girl who is a part of the whole episode is also a creature of fantasy, and the toys have no concrete existence, they are just symbols. The entire ballet is a dream world, and the choreographer's task has been to make us believe in the reality of that dream world. On paper the scenario makes no sense at all. This is ballet the farthest removed from literature. It succeeds because the relationship of music to movement and colour makes our imagination work. Put the story into a realistic setting and the whole thing would seem rubbish. Joan Miro's surrealist scene shows that ballet is an admirable medium for surrealist art. The fault in such a ballet as *Choreartium* is that the scenery is too static and reminiscent of actuality for the music. In *Jeux d'Enfants* music and scenery are more closely related than in any other contemporary work.

There is such a thing as narrative music that develops a plot; there is also music that paints various images and suggests an atmosphere, but that is never explicit. Both types of music are suitable to ballet, but only if the first is allied to a narrative and realistic décor, the second to a vague poetic idea and an imaginative setting. *Scheherazade* is an admirable example of the first, *Jeux d'Enfants* of the second. The second type might be said to belong to the " decadent " school, to borrow an analogy from poetry, where the music of words and the feelings induced by that music are the poet's aim and not the precise value of the words. An understanding of this would save many failures in ballets in which the music has not been specially commissioned.

Cotillon, Balanchine's ballet of about the same date, 1932, is also a notable example of the decadent school. A ball is in progress. Certain exciting things happen. We feel that they are affecting the lives of the dancers but cannot explain them. The ball continues, and finishes in a burst of gaiety, the central character turning like a top while the curtain falls. Was it an ordinary ball, or have we dreamed of the strange events? That is the first emotion we receive. The figures on the stage are utterly unreal; not the lovable, easy to describe characters of a *Boutique Fantasque*. But the creator's skill and consistency are such that we can readily believe in them.

Both these ballets were conceived by a poet, Boris Kochno, who excels in the " decadent " ballet.

(XIII) LA SYMPHONIE FANTASTIQUE

Five ballets in one

La Symphonie Fantastique was presented at Covent Garden in 1936 after many years' planning.

Although a choreographic version of Berlioz' *Symphony*, it did not arouse the customary controversy, since the composer himself laid down a programme and foresaw the possibility of its production in theatrical form.

Nothing shows Massine's versatility and skill better than this ballet in five parts, each part of which is a distinct ballet.

The first part is the true symphonic ballet of the *Choreartium* type, though there is no abstraction. In its grouping and pattern it reaches great heights, and it has a unity lacking in *Choreartium*, since all the action centres round the person of the Musician and seems to flow from him. Its faults are those inherent in symphonic ballet: certain beginnings and endings of movements and lifts for which the music has no equivalent and which suddenly jar and shock. The setting, by Bérard, immediately strikes the right romantic note, but the costumes again present a problem; those same draperies and tights that we have come to think of as " symphonic costume," which require bare feet, arms, and legs to be really in keeping.

The second movement, in the ballroom with its swirling couples waltzing, is more conventionally balletic, because the music is more definitely dance music. The scene is a beautiful and satisfying thing in itself, but it rather loses sight of the drama. The dance beguiles us so much that the quest of the Musician for his Beloved becomes a secondary matter. Ashton, who has treated the identical subject in *Apparitions*, has made his ballroom scene more moving by treating his whirling couples as a background to the drama.

The white costumes against the red colonnaded room are not merely striking in themselves, but belong to the ballet, a rarity in these works where the music dictates the whole manner.

The third movement presented the greatest problem of all, through both its length and its type. The first movement spoke of conflicting emotions, the second was a waltz; this third tells a story, but not in direct narrative. The Musician is feeling, groping his way. He has halted by a pastoral scene, beguiled by its serenity. He sees his ideal, but she is only an image. It is the last period of calm before the violence to come, and a hint of that violence is conveyed by the sudden gusts of wind. Listening to the music the problem of presenting parallel action to so ruminative a mood seems insoluble. Yet Massine has succeeded in creating some of the noblest choreography of this generation: the only pastoral ballet that is convincing. He has fully grasped the mood and attempts no direct narrative. The Musician is there, a passive figure, but one who dominates the action dramatically, though not physically. It is obvious that the action we are watching is being seen through his eyes and is closely related to his sorrows. When he leaves the stage nothing but the wind remains. In this scene Massine tells the whole story. It is complete in itself, a deeply moving study of artistic frustration.

The next scene, where the Musician who has murdered his Beloved is tried and executed, the famous death march, is the most obviously dramatic; the first to tell a direct narrative. Bérard, the painter, has collaborated admirably with Massine in presenting a period picture, the biting satire of Daumier. The judges are executioners, the executioners sadists. The Musician indicates that the suffering is moral as well as physical. This act treats social satire in very much the same manner as Kurt Jooss has done in *The Green Table*. It is a new departure in Russian Ballet.

The final act, a witches' sabbath, the struggle between Church and hell for the Musician's soul, is in some respects the weakest dramatically, though for complexity of detail and pattern it is worthy of a Breughel or Hieronymus Bosch. This scene, so much a set piece of the Romantic period, has been treated many times recently. Ashton was the first to do so in *Apparitions*; then Fokine in *Don Juan*; and Nijinska in *The Legend of Cracow*. Fokine's version was simpler and more immediately effective, because the eye could take in the whole at a first glance; but Massine has conveyed better than anyone the danger to the soul as apart from the danger to the body. The moment where the Beloved has turned into a witch is one of the most gruesome in all ballet. With repeated viewings this scene grows greatly in intensity, and the manner in which the choreographer has indicated the mediævalism of the Second Empire is an extraordinary *tour de force*.

La Symphonie Fantastique as a whole is a monumental work.

There is yet another group of works with which I propose to deal. They are in the repertoire of our national company at Sadler's Wells and have a considerable importance, not only because they are good in themselves, but because they are landmarks in the development of English Ballet. They may be considered standard works in the sense that I have been using the word. Other important works in this repertoire have already been dealt with in the sketches of their creators.

(XIV) JOB: THE RAKE'S PROGRESS:
BAR AUX FOLIES BERGÈRE
Inspiration from painting

Job, to music by Vaughan Williams, was created for the Camargo Society by Ninette de Valois. It is a smart thing to call this an admirable work and then to say, " but of course it is not a ballet." On the programme itself it is styled a masque, which is also inaccurate. Such nomenclature has very little importance, but it must be corrected or it leads us on a false trail. If *Job* is not a ballet, then there are only a score of ballets in existence today. There is an idea that ballet must consist of a series of set dances, and if those dances do not follow in quick succession and are not underlined so that the veriest tyro cannot miss them, it becomes the thing to say, " There is not enough dancing in this ballet."

Job is all dancing; movement guided by music is dancing and nothing else. It is essential to understand once and for all that in ballet, just as in opera, there is *aria* and *recitative*. *Job* has its grand aria, Satan's dance; it has magnificent choral passages, and it uses recitative.

It tells the story of *Job* in terms of Blake, an extremely risky thing that has here succeeded beyond a doubt. The work of a painter is static, the choreographer must make it move, but always in the spirit of the painter. He must, in fact, paint thousands of pictures in his manner. Already the nature of the art binds de Valois to the music; when she seeks pictorial inspiration she is bound to a series of paintings as well, greatly increasing the difficulty of the art. All choreographers have found inspiration in painting, but only occasional inspiration, not the idea for an entire work.

In *The Rake's Progress,* to specially written music by Gavin Gordon, de Valois has animated Hogarth's series of narrative pictures, perhaps a still more difficult task. Again she has succeeded in creating a truly English masterpiece. *The Rake's Progress,* while it has not the depth and pathos of the Russian masterpiece, is to English Ballet what *Petrouchka* is to Russian, a truly national expression.

In both these ballets de Valois reveals to an exceptional degree one of the indispensable assets of the choreographer, the ability to produce, an entirely different thing from creation. Production begins when creation has ceased.

The Rake's Progress is full of interesting characterisation brought out in dancing. Even its minor characters, such as the woman with the fan who visits the asylum in the final scene, are complete. There is no *corps de ballet*, but a company of *dancer-actors*. A work of this type is truly English, because the new English dancer, lacking an inherited tradition, excels where she can hide her lack of self-confidence behind a positive role. She has the technique for the classics, but has still to find a full measure of assurance. She can best express herself through the medium of another character. Gavin Gordon's score is an admirable example of well-composed narrative music perfectly suited to its subject.

De Valois has tried to animate yet a third picture, Manet's *Bar aux Folies Bergère,* and has failed, for a very positive reason. Success was impossible from the start. Manet is not telling a story. He is not interested in the life of his famous barmaid. What interests him is the solution of the problem of her colour and shape in relation to the bottles on the bar, the red triangle of Bass, the chandelier and the illumination. That problem he has solved, and the solution can have no possible relationship to ballet. It is as absolute as a vase of roses or a bowl of fruit by the same painter. There can be no question of carrying it a stage farther. The result is that her characters are unconvincing, vaguely reminiscent of another painter, Toulouse-Lautrec, but on the whole more suggestive of the Gay-Paree of the week-end visiting Englishman. No impressionist painter can possibly inspire ballet. The problem of being inspired by another medium, painting, is the same as in the choice of the music. It must be susceptible to *translation.*

(XV) CHECKMATE

Symbolism and realism

Checkmate, designed for the first visit of the Sadler's Wells Ballet to Paris and presented at the Champs Elysées in 1937, is the result of a long and close collaboration so characteristic of the work of Sadler's Wells today.

It tells the story of a symbolical game of chess played between Love and Death. The score, by Arthur Bliss, is descriptive and highly dramatic, though in its timing and at intervals in its volume it is conceived on an operatic rather than a balletic principle. De Valois introduces her players in a short scene clearly indicating the nature of the struggle, then the curtain rises on the chessboard and we see the preparations for war. The characters start as completely impersonal beings, very gradually gaining our sympathy as they assume personalities; until we take a vivid interest in the fortunes of the game, siding with the dotard Red King and his loving young wife and with their chivalrous champion Knight against the ruthless Judith-like Black Queen. De Valois has succeeded in conveying not only the tension of the game, but its ultimate import-ance, alternating hope and despair like a skilled teller of fables in the bazaar.

McKnight Kauffer's décor and costumes are among the most successful in modern ballet. The background shows up the movement, the scene helps to tell the story, the colour scheme echoes the dramatic intensity of the music. In conception the decoration is a skilful compromise be-tween reality and abstraction, just as the dancers are half puppet and half human; a method that suggests vast possi-bilities in bringing the scenic element back to its partner-ship in the whole.

(XVI) Façade

A burlesque

The *suite de danses* known as *Façade,* to music by William Walton, was created for the Camargo Society by Frederick Ashton in 1931. It proved immediately popu-lar, and was taken into the repertoire of the Ballet Club and of Sadler's Wells. It is performed several times every

season, and its continued success proves that the humour is not ephemeral.

Façade is a burlesque of dancing in terms of dancing. With extraordinary observation Ashton has seized upon the characteristics of various types of dance and has caricatured them to exactly the same degree that Walton has done in his music. Such a burlesque as apart from satire is a definitely English characteristic, and *Façade* is not an imitation Russian ballet, but a truly original contribution.

There is a tendency to decry all ballet that does not aim deliberately at beauty, and for that reason the merits of so light-hearted a work might easily be overlooked. There is no precedent to suggest that ballet cannot include burlesque, and there are accounts of burlesques in which the Kings of France took part. The burlesque is only bad if it is not " translated," and *Façade* is yet another striking example of the notion that I explained in the case of *The Three-cornered Hat*.

The Polka is the most stimulating and original when a classical dancer removes her skirt and performs a ridiculous little dance, but one that at the same time is extremely difficult. One says, in fact, " all this preparation and all this technique to express that! " and laughs, as one always does at pomposity and anti-climax. The tap-dance and the shooting dance belong to the humour of a Coward; the Waltz, with its focal point the legs, is a brilliant piece of observation.

(XVII) Les Patineurs: Les Rendezvous

Dancing for the sake of dancing—almost

Each of these ballets of Frederick Ashton's is connected by a slender idea; each one an admirable success because the medium has been handled with consummate tact.

Les Patineurs is the *translation* of skating in terms of ballet, a burlesque like *Façade,* but one which has as its object the revelation of an astonishing variety of virtuoso

AMBROSE

Les Patineurs

technique. To burlesque skating alone might be ingenious, but it would soon become monotonous. While Ashton has been consistent and has never allowed us to forget that the dancers are on ice, he has made each dance technically exciting in itself. Meyerbeer's music is simple, Ashton's action is complex, with the result that we can take it all in at a glance. So skilfully interwoven are his dances, so rapidly do they succeed one another, that what might be a *suite de danses* is actually a ballet. The drama is in the action and not in the idea. The audience asks the question: " What is going to happen next? " The result is the exceedingly brilliant handling of classicism: dancing for the sake of dancing—almost. And the *almost* gives it a character that makes it acceptable to a modern audience.

Les Rendezvous is also a ballet entirely composed of *arias*. Its theme is brilliantly simple, meetings and partings, and admirably suited to Auber's music. It would be difficult to imagine a theme that could be more directly conveyed in movement or that could link one dance to the next in such logical and rapid succession. Remove the connecting link and the result is a competent commonplace.

In these ballets Ashton challenges the Russians on their own ground, using his dancers with no character disguise.

For both these works William Chappell, a dancer, has devised settings and costumes that are highly effective.

(XVIII) HOROSCOPE

The triumph of collaboration

Horoscope is a finely planned work, a close collaboration in the Diaghileff sense of the word. The subject of a couple separated and then united by their guiding stars was conceived by the composer, Constant Lambert. It is simple and easily told in movement. He starts with a short introduction, monotonous and mathematical, a fine piece of theatre that makes the spectator concentrate, paving the way for a violent opening. Ashton, the choreographer, has taken full advantage of every opportunity, contrasting the violent and the tender, blending them and ending on a triumphantly tender note. Sophie Fedorovitch, who has designed the settings and costumes, has, like Ashton, been closely guided by the music. There is one moment in which the unity of idea is particularly striking: when, ushered in by the brass, the violent characters in red invade the calm, pale characters with irresistible force, forming a pattern of moving beauty. In this work Ashton for the first time uses a *corps de ballet* with as much force and originality as he does his leading dancers, and shows a complete mastery of the medium.

(XIX) The Wise and Foolish Virgins

Painting and music meet

This is a work of extraordinary serenity and completeness, the creation of a mature choreographer. In it he tells the parable as seen through Renaissance eyes, and his use of Italian painting is both sure and subtle. It has been completely translated for the stage. There is no insistence on the easily composed and easily identified *tableau vivant*. From the moment that he created the slight but charming *Florentine Picture*, Ashton has been preparing himself for this. Always happy in the *pas de deux*, here he handles the whole composition with mastery.

I wrote that the inspiration was pictorial; that is only half the truth. It is equally musical. The movement and unfolding of the narrative flow directly from the Bach music so brilliantly arranged and orchestrated by William Walton. Ashton has provided the perfect meeting-place for music and painting. That is the ideal of ballet, the perfect fusion of the arts composing it.

Once again Ashton shows himself in the great tradition of Fokine—telling his story entirely in movement, building his characterisation through movement, and placing no

emphasis on facial expression. In this he differs from the
direction that British choreography seems to be taking.

(XX) DANTE SONATA

A ballet of actuality

This powerful work shows Ashton in a new mood. We
have seen his wit and humour, his elegance, his serenity.
This is a ballet as much inspired by the contemporary
scene as Jooss' *Green Table,* but less direct in its presentation. Jooss shows us irony and satire, Ashton horror and
compassion. We have already had a glimpse of that
Ashton in *Horoscope.* This is a perfectly controlled work
of passionate intensity. It gives the lie to those who dis-
miss ballet as escapism and deny that it can comment on
actuality. It can and does, but subtly. None of these
characters bears the label " Poland " or " Democracy "
or " Totalitarianism," but there is little doubt of Ashton's
meaning from the rise of the curtain till the unforgettable
final tableau when good as well as evil find nothing but
suffering. Such a ballet cannot be translated into words,
it is the farthest removed from literature, but there is no
mistaking the emotions that it inspires.

(XXI) HAMLET

The choreographer as literary critic

This is Robert Helpmann's second ballet, following the
successful *Comus,* in which he wedded the masque and the
ballet, poetry and the dance, with a considerable measure
of success.

Helpmann has taken a literary subject; but as a great
" theatreman " has avoided the many and obvious pitfalls
and has remained true to his medium. Others have taken
Shakespeare for reasons I have never understood, and have
told the stories of the selected plays, usually inadequately.
One can only ask oneself: Why? Why? When Shake-

speare has done so to perfection! Why? When the story itself is of no importance, when it was already second or third hand! When Shakespeare gave it life and beauty!

Helpmann has done nothing of the kind, he has given us the choreographer's comment on Hamlet, a very different matter. He shows us what goes on in Hamlet's mind when, like a drowning man, his life passes in review through his fevered and dying brain. He has shown us this, as he can in his medium, by a series of images that interpret the story according to modern psychology. He does not insist or elaborate, but présents these images dramatically. This is literary criticism perfectly *translated* into ballet, and as such it is an entirely new departure.

One must mention the important role that Leslie Hurry's costumes and décor play in completing the work and making it a whole. They are the link between Tchaikovsky's romanticism and Helpmann's modern viewpoint.

.   .   .   .   .   .

The ballet at Sadler's Wells, as the commentary on these and other works, all of them recent, so clearly indicates, shows a knowledge both of the traditions and of the nature of ballet that seems in danger of being forgotten by the Russians of today. A ballet is made or destroyed by its initial conception. It must be insisted upon once again: Music, idea, choreography, decoration must express each in its own way and together a common idea.

(XXII) MIRACLE IN THE GORBALS

Characterisation in the round

For a number of reasons this must rank as one of the outstanding creations of contemporary ballet. It dares more than other works; its success is all the greater. The story is the popular one of the return of the Saviour to the modern scene. It is obviously dramatic, but presents many dangers from offensive bad taste to mawkishness. It is a tribute to the success of the ballet that the highest praise has come from the religious press. The setting for this visitation is the Gorbals in Glasgow. This is a singularly happy choice, enabling the choreographer to probe behind the Palais de Danse atmosphere of the crowded city slum on a Saturday night and to find the true emotional depths of these people in their national Scottish dances. Arthur Bliss has written a brilliant score on those lines, making full use of natural sounds, such as the wailing of a ship's siren, and also of Scottish national music. The result is not a sordid slum picture but a sympathetic study that presents people as they really are, that looks under the surface and can rise to lyrical heights. One of the most moving moments in the whole of ballet occurs when the stranger brings the young suicide to life. At first she still belongs to the world of the spirit, then gradually as the blood warms within her she breaks into some country dance remembered from childhood. The parson who opposes and finally brings about the death of the stranger is no mere villain but a complex personality, capable of great good as well as evil. For the first time this is characterisation in the round; these are not puppets but living people. There are two directions that Helpmann might have taken but has not: the impression of a big city, already brilliantly done by Jooss, or the presentation of a social problem, also within the province of Jooss. What he has done is to say, " Here are a mass of people in a sordid slum. They all look more or less the same. How do they react both as individuals and as a group in a particular emergency? " The ballet is a working out of that, done with great directness but with a sublety that gradually reveals itself. These tough dwellers in the dockland slum are suddenly moved by the primitive fear of a mountain people when confronted with death.

In this modern miracle play Helpmann, Bliss, and the painter Burra have introduced something new to ballet.

(XXIII) THE GREEN TABLE

A major work outside the Russian tradition

I include one ballet outside the Russian tradition because it is a work of outstanding merit, of continued topical interest that has been applauded throughout the whole civilised world, the Fascist countries excluded.

Kurt Jooss and his group of dancers from Essen first came into prominence when they won the first prize in the choreographic competition inaugurated by Les Archives Internationales de la Danse. The prize-winning work was *The Green Table*, and though Kurt Jooss has since produced many ballets of considerable merit, he remains the creator of one work, the justification for the existence of the group and for its world travels.

The Green Table is a powerful indictment of the failure of the League of Nations. The curtain rises on an international conference, the senile senators talk, quarrel, shots are exchanged, and then we are shown what happens when Death is let loose. The curtain falls on a repetition of the first act, platitudes, arguments, and shots. Since its creation *The Green Table* has become more and more topical.

Kurt Jooss has evolved a technique of his own, a blend of the Central European methods of Laban with a foundation of ballet technique. His company can boast the most perfect *ensemble* of any today—lightness, musicality, and precision. His fault seems to be his unwillingness to take the fullest advantage of ballet technique. Such a man has the unique opportunity of being able to add much that is valuable to the old system and to use it in new ways. His most expressive scenes in *The Green Table* are the first and last, where the dancers are deliberately limited in movement by their seated positions round the table. Where they are allowed full movement one feels the limitations imposed by his system. Jooss, using ballet technique plus what he has shown us he could add, should be the creator of a series of effective ballets, instead of justly famed as the creator of one great imaginative work.

Details of the Works commented on in this Chapter

Giselle: a ballet in two acts by Théophile Gautier and the Chevalier de Saint-Georges after a suggestion by Heine. Choreography by Coralli, music by Adolph Adam. Created in 1841, with Carlotta Grisi as Giselle. Revived by Diaghileff in 1911 for Karsavina and Nijinsky. Danced by Pavlova, Spessivtseva, Markova, Fonteyn.

The Swan Lake: a ballet in four acts by Modeste Tchaikovsky. Choreography by Petipa and Ivanoff. First performed in 1877. Revived in 1894 with Legnani in the leading role. Has been danced by all the leading Russian *ballerinas*. Revived by Diaghileff in various abbreviated forms, the best known being a one-act version consisting mainly of Act II of the original. Given in full at Sadler's Wells.

Aurora's Wedding: a one-act abbreviation of *The Sleeping Princess*. Choreography by Petipa, music by Tchaikovsky. The original work given at the Maryinsky in 1890, with Carlotta Brianza as the Princess, Aurora and Cecchetti as the Blue Bird and the Fairy Carabosse. Revived by Diaghileff at the Alhambra in 1921, with Trefilova, Egorova, Spessivtseva, and Lopokova alternating as *ballerina*. Presented in one act in Paris, 1922. Revived by de Basil in 1935.

Les Sylphides: a romantic reverie in one act by Michael Fokine to music by Chopin. Created as *Chopiniana* for a charity fête in 1908. Presented by Diaghileff the following year. In the repertoire of every ballet company today.

Le Spectre de la Rose: choreographic poem in one act by Jean Louis Vandoyer after a poem by Gautier. Produced by Diaghileff in 1910, with Karsavina and Nijinsky. In every repertoire today.

Carnaval: a ballet in one act by Fokine, choreography by Fokine, music by Schumann. Décor and costumes by

Bakst. Composed for a charity, then presented by Diaghileff in 1910, with Nijinsky as Harlequin. In every repertoire today.

Scheherazade: a ballet in one act by Michael Fokine. Choreography by Fokine, music by Rimsky-Korsakov, décors and costumes by Bakst. Presented by Diaghileff in 1910. Original cast: Ida Rubinstein as Zobeide, Nijinsky as the Golden Slave. Zobeide subsequently taken by Karsavina. Revived by de Basil, 1935; René Blum, 1936.

Thamar: a ballet in one act by Fokine after Lermontov's poem. Choreography by Fokine, music by Balakirev, décors and costumes by Bakst. Produced in 1912 by Diaghileff. Original cast: Karsavina as Thamar, Bolm as the Prince. Revived by de Basil, 1935.

Prince Igor: the Polovtsian dances to Borodin's opera. Choreography by Fokine, décor and costumes originally by Roerich. Another version by Korovin, presented by Diaghileff in 1909, with Adolph Bolm in the leading role, maintained in the repertoire ever since. Given by de Basil, René Blum, and Léon Woizikowski.

Petrouchka: dance drama in four scenes by Alexandre Benois and Michael Fokine. Choreography by Fokine, music by Stravinsky, décors and costumes by Benois. First presented by Diaghileff in 1911. Original cast: Karsavina, the Dancer; Nijinsky, Petrouchka; Orloff, the Moor. Revived by de Basil, 1922, René Blum, and Léon Woizikowski.

L'Épreuve d'Amour: a ballet in one act by André Derain and Michael Fokine; choreography by Fokine, music by Mozart, décor and costumes by Derain. Presented by René Blum in 1936, with Nemtchinova as Chung Yang, Eglevsky as the Lover, Yazvinsky as the Mandarin.

The Three-cornered Hat: a ballet in one act by Martinez Sierra, after a story by Alarcon. Choreography by Massine, music by da Falla, décor and costumes and dropcurtain by Picasso. Presented by Diaghileff in 1919, with

Karsavina and Massine. Revived by de Basil, 1934, with Toumanova and Massine.

La Boutique Fantasque: a ballet in one act, with choreography by Massine, music by Rossini, arranged and orchestrated by Respighi. Décor, costumes, and drop-curtains by Derain. Presented by Diaghileff in 1919, with Lopokova and Massine as the can-can dancèrs. Revived by de Basil in 1935 with Danilova and Massine.

Le Beau Danube: a ballet in one act by Massine. Choreography by Massine, music by Johann Strauss, costumes by Étienne de Beaumont, décor by Polunin after Guys. First produced for Étienne de Beaumont in 1923 with Lopokova, Marra, and Massine. Revived by de Basil in a new form with Danilova, Riabouchinska, and Massine, 1933.

Jeux d'Enfants: a ballet in one act by Boris Kochno. Choreography by Massine, music by Bizet, décor, costumes, and drop-curtain by Miro. Presented by de Basil in 1932, with Toumanova as the Top, Riabouchinska as the Child, Lichine as the Traveller, Woizikowski as the Sportsman.

Cotillon: a ballet in one act by Boris Kochno. Choreography by Balanchine, music by Chabrier, décor by Bérard. Produced for de Basil in 1932, with Toumanova, Woizikowski, Lichine, and Rostova.

La Symphonie Fantastique: choreographic symphony in five scenes. Music and theme by Berlioz, choreography by Massine, décor and costumes by Bérard. Produced for de Basil in 1936, with Toumanova as the Beloved, Massine as the Musician.

Job: a masque for dancing in eight scenes by Geoffrey Keynes from the Biblical story. Music by Vaughan Williams, décor and costumes after Blake by G. Raverat, masks by Hedley Briggs. Choreography by Ninette de Valois. Produced for the Camargo Society in 1931, now in Sadler's Wells repertoire. Anton Dolin as Satan; in revivals, Robert Helpmann.

The Rake's Progress: a ballet in six scenes by Gavin Gordon (after Hogarth). Music by Gavin Gordon, choreography by de Valois, décor and costumes by Rex Whistler (after Hogarth). Produced in 1935 with Walter Gore as the Rake, Markova as the Girl. Revived with Robert Helpmann and Elizabeth Miller.

Bar aux Folies Bergère: a one-act ballet by Ninette de Valois. Choreography by de Valois, décor and costumes by William Chappell. Ballet Club production in 1934. Markova as La Goulue.

Checkmate: a ballet in a prologue and one scene by Arthur Bliss. Choreography by Ninette de Valois, décor and costumes by McKnight Kauffer. Produced at Sadler's Wells in 1937 with June Brae as the Black Queen, Pamela May as the Red Queen, Robert Helpmann as the Red King, Harold Turner as the Red Knight.

Façade: suite de danses in one act by William Walton. Choreography by Frederick Ashton, music by William Walton, décor and costumes by John Armstrong. Camargo Society production in 1931, with Lopokova as the Milkmaid, Markova in the Polka.

Les Patineurs: a ballet in one act with music by Meyerbeer, selected by Constant Lambert. Choreography by Frederick Ashton, décor and costumes by William Chappell. Sadler's Wells, 1937, with Harold Turner, Mary Honer, Elizabeth Miller, June Brae, Pamela May, and Margot Fonteyn.

Les Rendezvous: a ballet in one act with music by Auber (selected by Constant Lambert). Choreography by Ashton, décor and costumes (two versions) by William Chappell. Sadler's Wells, 1935.

Horoscope: a ballet in three scenes by Constant Lambert. Music by Constant Lambert, choreography by Frederick Ashton, décor and costumes by Fedorovitch. Margot Fonteyn and Michael Somes, the Lovers; Richard Ellis and Alan Carter, the Twins; Pamela May, the Moon.

The Wise and Foolish Virgins: music from Bach, orchestrated by William Walton. Décors by Rex Whistler, choreography by Frederick Ashton. Created at Sadler's Wells, 1939.

The Dante Sonata: music by Liszt. Décors by Sophie Fedorovitch, choreography by Frederick Ashton. Created at Sadler's Wells, 1940.

Hamlet: music by Tchaikovsky. Décors by Leslie Hurry, choreography by Robert Helpmann. Created at the New Theatre, 1943.

Miracle in the Gorbals: ballet by M. Bentall. Music by Arthur Bliss, décors by Edward Burra, choreography by Robert Helpmann. Created at Princes Theatre, October 26, 1944.

Other important works are discussed under different headings.

CHAPTER 7

Appreciation : Studies of some Contemporary Dancers

(*A practical application of Chapter Three*)

I HAVE purposely kept any reference to the dancers themselves out of the main body of the text, so as not to con-
fuse criticism with personalities; also such matter rapidly
dates and needs constant revision. The modern critical
tendency has been to stress the role of the performers at
the expense of a clear view of the art as a whole. Also,
in any writing on young dancers the critic is faced with a
grave difficulty, since the young dancer of today who
usually makes a name while she is still immature mentally
and physically varies almost from performance to performance. There is an awkward age between fifteen and
eighteen during which the young dancer must adjust herself. She owes her first success to youthful charm and
intuition. Will she succeed as a conscious artist? I have
seen many promising dancers disappear during this awkward age. A knowledge of diet and hygiene would be of
the greatest value in assisting the body in adapting itself
to a difficult life.

The critic who shows any enthusiasm at all and who
does not continually hedge must inevitably be accused of
a lack of consistency, especially by those actively in the
movement themselves. It is far easier to think that the
critic has shifted his ground than to see that one has failed
to make progress. The critic cannot continually be throw-
ing cold water on young dancers, and owes it to his public
to risk prophecies.

However, risk or no risk, a study such as this to be
complete must contain some account of the leading dancers of today, especially since the historical section has
shown us the enormous influence of the individual dancer

on the art as a whole. A dancer may exert such an influence perfectly unconsciously and without the possession of exceptional artistry. The type of Ida Rubinstein, not a classically trained dancer at all, undoubtedly inspired both Fokine and Bakst to create a series of exotic ballets.

Just as I have judged the ballets in the last chapter through the standards laid down in my æsthetic background, so have I judged the dancers. It has obviously been impossible to include every dancer of note, and I do not pretend that this is a complete list of the best dancers of the day, certainly not of all those whose work interests me. I have included those whose progress best illustrates some particular point that has already been discussed.

The case of the young English dancers is especially interesting and important, since their progress has been normal, and we are no longer accustomed to normal progress in ballet, but to jerky ups and downs, caused by unsuitable work and excess of work. Each of these dancers represented a problem in education, solved, not by chance, but by the finest system of education in ballet to-day.

There is as yet no clearly defined English school and therefore no marked difference between the best of the English and the best of the Russian dancers. The difference can be seen through a study of the average, the small *soliste* and the *corps de ballet* dancer. The average Russian is markedly superior in everything save the neat and correct execution of steps. She has more self-confidence, more to express, and a greater sense of the stage. If her technique is untidy, she is more of a dancer, and she can finish her sequence of steps with a strong climax. The average English dancer is still repressed by the nature of her education, the good old slogans of " play the game," " sink yourself in the team," " it's bad form to show off "; and " showing off " is the very thing she must do.

One of the reasons for the extraordinary success of the Wells and Ballet Club schools in turning out personalities lies in the fact that the stage is there the whole time, the sole aim of the pupils, instead of examinations or the vague hope of getting into some show or other.

(A) In Russian Ballet

(I) *Alexandra Danilova*

Alexandra Danilova is the most finished dancer of our period, the last of a certain type of stylist trained through the bounty of a court and not with haphazard speed. Her grounding has been so thorough that she has been able to improve as an artist steadily but perceptibly since she has been a *prima ballerina*.

Danilova first came to London in 1924 with Georges Balanchine and a small group, calling themselves the Russian State Dancers. She joined the Diaghileff Ballet the following year, and soon became the last *ballerina* of the company.

When the de Basil Ballet was formed, she was young enough to fit in with his policy of youth, old enough to be a link with the past. Her work has been, not only of the greatest value in itself, but also as an example to the young dancers of the company.

Danilova has not a wide emotional range, but her sense of style and stagecraft, her pure classicism, and her ideal build, with the magnificently straight knees of the *ballerina,* allow her considerable versatility in roles of nobility or light humour, from the uncompromising classicism of *The Swan Lake* to the sparkling *soubrette* roles in *Le Beau Danube, La Boutique Fantasque,* and *The Good-humoured Ladies.* She is the only dancer in the revival of this last ballet to capture the delicate-period style.

Her technique is not that of a virtuoso, but it is so well subordinated to the roles she interprets that one does not think of her in terms of technique. Today she remains faithful to ballet.

(II) *Irina Baronova*

Baronova is the type of modern classical dancer with a wide emotional range and beautiful fluidity of movement. Her parents settled in Rumania during the early days of the Russian Revolution, and she received her first lessons there. At about the age of nine she came to Paris to study with Preobrajenska. Her first engagement was at the age of twelve, at the Mogador, in Offenbach's *Orphée aux Enfers* in a ballet arranged by Balanchine. She immediately attracted critical attention. She joined de Basil in 1932, becoming a *ballerina* in 1933 when the company came to the Alhambra. On the first night she appeared in *Les Sylphides, Les Présages,* and *Le Beau Danube,* showing an extraordinary versatility and a brilliantly easy technique. She was largely responsible for the historic success of that first season, a success that launched *balletomania* in England. As an actress she has shone in such roles as Lady Gay in *Union Pacific,* the midinette in *Le Beau Danube,* and most especially as the Queen of Shemakhan in *Le Coq d'Or,* a role of great length and complexity.

After an interruption to her career through ill-health, Baronova is now dancing in musical comedy.

(III) *Tamara Toumanova*

It is Toumanova who more than anyone launched the idea of the baby *ballerina.*

She was born in Russia during the Revolution; her parents escaped through Siberia to Shanghai. After seeing Pavlova she determined to become a dancer. She went to Paris at the age of seven and learnt with Preobrajenska. At the age of nine she appeared at the Opéra, Paris, as a guest artist, and later kept herself by giving dance recitals. Discovered by Balanchine, she joined de Basil in 1932, creating three outstanding roles in *Concurrence, Cotillon,* and *Jeux d'Enfants,* in which her *fouettés* caused a sensation that played a great role in popularising the young ballet and sending children to the dance studios. At the same time she appeared in revivals of standard works. In 1933 she left de Basil to appear with *Les Ballets,* 1933, returning to him later in the year.

Toumanova is outstandingly beautiful, with a very strong technique that she is inclined to force at times. She is a classical dancer who at her best can give a memorable performance in *Aurora's Wedding,* and a character dancer who has appeared in *The Three-cornered Hat* with success. It is Balanchine, however, who has understood her the best, building roles round her physique and personality.

Toumanova has unquestionably played a major role amongst contemporary dancers.

She is now acting on the films, but also continues her career in ballet.

(IV) *Tatiana Riabouchinska*

Of all the young dancers Riabouchinska is unquestionably the most individual.

Her mother was a dancer, and she is the only second-generation dancer of her group. She learned in Paris from Volinine and then Kchesinska, and joined the Balieff Chauve-Souris, with whom she toured. She joined de Basil in 1932.

Riabouchinska is not a purely classical dancer, lacking the necessary hardness and attack. She is in no sense a character dancer and, save in *Les Sylphides,* not a romantic. It is, indeed, difficult to attach to her any label. She has almost launched a style. She is incredibly light, with a fine elevation and beautiful arms, the very reverse of a *terre-à-terre* dancer. Her personality, too, is such that she excels in roles that are gay or fey, as the Butterfly in *Carnaval,* Frivolity in *Les Présages,* or the Child in *Jeux d'Enfants.* Her gaiety is not that of the *soubrette*, it is something far more intangible. One associates her with

183

birds and butterflies. She glitters rather than glows. Her technique is not always precise, but it is invariably effective. After an absence of many years from London she is the one whose work remains the most vividly in one's memory.

She has recently been dancing in operette.

(v) *Nina Verchinina*

Nina Verchinina has not been seen very often of late, but she is a dancer of considerable importance, more closely associated with the roles she has created than any other dancer save Riabouchinska.

For certain parts of his symphonies, the most symphonic in structure, Massine needed a certain type of dancer, classically trained but part Duncan. In Nina Verchinina, classicism and the type of dancing that is called Central European have met, showing the value of the classical grounding and the value of points in accentuating, not lightness this time, but the strength of steel. As Action in *Les Présages* and in the second part of *Choreartium*, Verchinina has created a new type, a fact that can be fully appreciated when we see the same roles competently performed, but without the musical subtlety and understanding that informs them and that makes one talk of a Verchinina role, in spite of all rules to the contrary.

(vi) *Alicia Markova*

Markova was the first child prodigy in Russian Ballet. She learnt from the late Seraphine Astafieva, and, after various commercial engagements, joined the Diaghileff Ballet in 1925 at the age of fourteen, dancing the *adagio* of *The Swan Lake* the same year. For Diaghileff she created the Nightingale, danced the Cat, and the Blue Bird.

After Diaghileff's death she undertook many commercial engagements, and danced with the young English Ballet at the Camargo Society, the Ballet Club, Sadler's Wells, and with her own company.

Markova is, in physique and temperament, a truly

classical dancer in the direct line of Pavlova and Spessiva, though technically she has less finish and emotionally her range is smaller. She is light, precise, and magnificently competent in everything she undertakes. A lack of guidance during the last few years has robbed her of a certain grandeur of style, and has tended to betray her into mannerisms which careful handling can soon eradicate.

Within clearly defined limits, she is classical and modern rather than romantic; she occupies a unique position in contemporary ballet, and has already played a major role in the history of the art in England.

Since the war Markova has been dancing with The Ballet Theatre in America. She has greatly added to her reputation and to the reputation of classical ballet in that country.

(VII) *David Lichine*

David Lichine first attracted attention in the Ida Rubinstein Company, where he came under the influence of Nijinska. He joined the de Basil Ballet in 1932.

He is a dancer of outstanding talent, requiring the discipline of a Cecchetti to do himself full justice. By temperament he is not a classical dancer, but at times he succeeds in classical roles, and there is always something interesting in what he does, even when he breaks through the rigid classical reserve. Lichine is at his best in romantic or character roles, in anything that exploits vitality and robustness rather than subtlety. At his worst he can be flamboyant in the extreme. At a time when few male dancers have a positive personality, such a dancer is of the greatest importance. He has much to say, and if he perfects his manner of presentation, he will rank high among contemporary influences on the dance.

Lichine has recently been producing ballet for the films as well as for the ballet, and has been appearing in some of those films. His work in this medium is competent, but remains filmed ballet rather than ballet for the films.

(VIII) *Nana Gollner*

Nana Gollner, a Hollywood girl with a film contract, studied with Theodor Kosloff. She joined the de Basil Ballet and then left to dance ballerina roles for René Blum. She is at present ballerina for the de Basil company.

She has a magnificent, easy technique and the true ballerina physique. Her dancing in *The Swan Lake* is one of the outstanding performances of the day.

(B) IN ENGLISH BALLET

(I) *Pearl Argyle*

Although Pearl Argyle has retired, this account of her work (1938) is retained, because she has played a major role in the popularisation of British ballet, as an English not an Anglo-Russian dancer.

Pearl Argyle was the first English dancer to make a name as such. She started her training late with Marie Rambert, who launched her at the Ballet Club; danced at the Camargo Society, with Balanchine in *Les Ballets*, 1933, and at Sadler's Wells.

Great physical beauty has been both an asset and a handicap, since it has often obscured very real gifts. Pearl Argyle was limited in technique and in range of expression, but within her limits her work showed that she understood herself; she was a truly finished artist, mature and serene, but not cold. Where her technique failed in the virtuoso roles, she could often save herself by her stagecraft. Her walk before the *adagio,* revealing moment, immediately convinced the audience of her grasp.

(II) *Margot Fonteyn*

Margot Fonteyn is the first *ballerina* to be produced by the National Ballet at Sadler's Wells.

She started her dancing in Shanghai, studied for a short time with Astafieva, and then joined the school at Sadler's Wells, of which she is the product. Her first role was in a revival of Ashton's *Rio Grande*. When Markova left the company, she inherited many of her roles.

Fonteyn is ideally built, an essentially intelligent dancer with rare musicality. She has progressed from a slow, dreamy, eternal Sylphide mood into an intensity of attack that has opened to her every role in the classical repertoire. Together with Baronova, she has the greatest range in contemporary ballet, from the sparkle of *The Swan Lake*, Act III, with its thirty-two *fouettés*, to the pure romance of *Les Sylphides* and the modern sophistication of *A Wedding Bouquet*. In *Giselle* she gives the most outstanding performance to be seen in ballet today: deeply emotional, but always controlled by the rigid period framework.

During the war years Fonteyn has created many important roles in *The Wanderer, The Wise Virgins, Dante Sonata, Hamlet, Comus*, and has given a memorable interpretation of Swanhilda in *Coppelia*. Free of all mannerisms, she has become a *ballerina assoluta*.

Margot Fonteyn is a striking example of the working of Sadler's Wells, both as a school and as a company, where careful handling develops all that is best in the artist. She is a born dancer, but she has been studied and developed from season to season with the greatest care. The Sadler's Wells system, a version of the old Russian system adapted to present-day needs and economics, can alone develop a fully matured company.

(III) *Pamela May*

Pamela May is a pure classical dancer with a fine line. She has created many roles with success, among them the Red Queen in *Checkmate*, the Moon in *Horoscope* and the dancer in *The Prospect before Us*. She has danced *Swan Lake* with the rather rare understanding that it is not *Les Sylphides* and has given a delightfully understanding interpretation of Swanhilda.

(IV) *Robert Helpmann*

Today there are few male dancers in the ballet schools, and the male dancer, however inadequate, receives work whether he has value as an artist or not. Robert Helpmann is a magnificent exception, and would be an outstanding artist at any period.

Born in Adelaide, he studied in Australia under the influence of Pavlova, and came to England as a pupil of the Wells school. Within a short time he was dancing leading roles.

Without an extraordinary technique he is incapable of making an ungraceful movement, a fact that reveals first-class teaching. He has a strong personality, but so perfectly disciplined that he is able to make a personal success, yet to remain in the framework of the ballet as a whole and to carry out the choreographer's intentions as few prominent dancers can do. This ability is characteristic of English dancing today. Perfectly musical, he is a perfect partner, for partnering is a question of ear as well as of strength and good manners. His range is enormous: classical, romantic, broad farce, or subtle comedy. He shares with Massine alone the ultimate secret of true art in dancing, the ability to give positive value to a static pose.

The essence of Helpmann's work is his extraordinary intelligence and the fact that he is a born " theatre man." Since the war he has turned choreographer, has acted Hamlet, has broadcast, and appeared in the films. Ballet needs this all-round ability, and since the time of Noverre has tended to lose sight of the fact that ballet is the basis of all theatre.

The Wells has been fortunate in its material, but that so young a company could develop two of the outstanding dancers of our day, a Fonteyn and a Helpmann, shows the value of the school.

(v) *Harold Turner*

Harold Turner started dancing in the Midlands, coming to Marie Rambert in London, who taught and produced him. One of his first important engagements was to dance as partner to Karsavina.

Turner is a magnificent technician and a truly virile personality, an example to the majority of young dancers. He is a classical dancer of the old type rather than the new, the true *premier danseur,* brilliant rather than lyrical, but he has a wide enough range to be excellent in character and broad comedy: the Farmer in *Barabau,* the Tap Dancer in *Façade.* Such an artist illustrates better than anyone my remarks on male dancing,[1] and should do much to remove the national prejudice against male dancers. Whether romantically clad or not, his masculinity is a positive contribution to the orchestration of dancing.

During the war Turner was dancing with the International Ballet. He has now returned to Sadler's Wells.

(VI) *Beryl Grey*

Outstanding among the younger dancers is the seventeen-year-old Beryl Grey, a product of the Sadler's Wells School. She is a classical dancer with a fluent technique and with very considerable natural grace. She has danced *The Swan Lake* with a brio that ranks her with the Baronovas and Toumanovas of the same age, and has doubled in many of Fonteyn's roles. It is early as yet to discuss her interpretations, which are always pleasing and unforced, but if she can overcome the difficult years that have destroyed so many promising dancers—and there are signs that she will—Sadler's Wells will have produced another ballerina.

(VII) *Sally Gilmour*

Marie Rambert is without doubt a great creator; one has only to glance at her record. She creates, not ballets, but the material for ballet—dances, choreographers, and scenic

[1] See page 147.

artists. There is no company today, Russian or English, that does not owe her a large debt.

After having lost many of her "creations" to other companies she has built anew, and Sally Gilmour succeeds Pearl Argyle, Maude Lloyd, and Rambert's other jewels. She made her name in Andrée Howard's *Lady into Fox* with a performance of rare interpretative skill. Gilmour shows intelligence and quality in all her work.

(VIII) *Other Dancers in English Ballet*

Never has the native ballet scene shown more promise. The English corps de ballet, noted in the past for discipline rather than personality, has developed with the opportunities afforded by the war. It is difficult to mention names, if such a record is not to become dated within a very short time, but there are many now who compel mention: Margaret Dale, a brilliant executant and a personality; Joan Sheldon, reminiscent of the great Sokolova in her attack; Pauline Clayden, who has real quality (her interpretation of the suicide in *Miracle in the Gorbals* is outstanding); Julia Farron, an artist of real individuality, whose Estrella in *Carnaval* is admirable, Moyra Fraser, Celia França, and Moira Shearer, an exceptionally intelligent dancer, who is proving herself to be more than a beauty.

Of necessity the male dancers have suffered and the original male members of Sadler's Wells are in the Forces. But admirable work has been done by David Paltenghi, the type of *danseur noble* but with an intelligence that gives him a wider scope; Alexis Rassine, who only needs the experience to become outstanding, and Gordon Hamilton.

Since the last edition of this book many prominent dancers have retired or have left Sadler's Wells, among them June Brae, Elizabeth Miller, and Mary Honer. Their outstanding work has added to the tradition that is making our national ballet into an artistic force of major importance.

Ballet 1939 — 1944: A Précis of Development

(i) THE NATIONAL BALLET

DURING the war years, and in spite of the innumerable material difficulties, the Sadler's Wells company has proved itself a National Ballet. I have dealt with that aspect at considerable length in another work,[1] and it is only necessary here to take a hurried glance at the record. It amply confirms what I originally wrote in the body of the text about the soundness of the Wells planning.

The first consideration is the school. It has now been in existence long enough to pay a handsome dividend: 75 per cent. of the personnel of the company were trained in its own school. This means a uniformity of style without which a ballet company cannot exist as a distinct personality. Diaghileff's strongest period was when the majority of his dancers were trained at the Imperial Theatre schools. There has never been a lack of dancers in Britain; there was the lack of a style that makes ballet truly national. The school ensures permanence and is a national asset of very great value. In time to come it will attract pupils from all over the world. Its problem will be to develop a balanced curriculum that can, as in Russia, take care of the dancer's general education. The authorities are keenly aware of that problem.

During the period under review the Wells has shown creations by four choreographers: Ashton, de Valois, Helpmann, and Andrée Howard. It is particularly fortunate that Howard, creator of *Death and the Maiden* and *Lady into Fox,* should have had the opportunity of producing on a large scale. Her delicate sensibility needed this spur.

[1] *The National Ballet.* (Black, 1943.)

Judged by any standards seen in London since 1933, Sadler's Wells has proved itself the peer of the very best; and as this development has been planned, marking a gradual advance from season to season, there can be no doubt that at last, after a long history as an appreciative audience, this country has a true ballet tradition. Ninette de Valois has earned the right to rank with the great artistic creators, and that without mentioning either the obvious or the hidden obstacles of these war years.

(ii) MARIE RAMBERT

After a not altogether happy period at the Arts Theatre in conjunction with other companies, and then an interval, Marie Rambert, pioneer of ballet in this country, has been able to re-form her company and to appear for C.E.M.A., in her own Mercury Theatre, and this is important. One is apt to write of Marie Rambert in the past, to acknowledge her work as the inspirer of Ashton, Argyle, and many others, and to leave it at that. Rambert, as an inspiring personality ever on the lookout for talent to develop, has a major part to play. Both by temperament, culture, and through the smaller scale on which she works she is admirably situated to experiment, to prevent ballet becoming too settled in its ways. There can be no school for choreographers; there can be a choreographic nursery, and Rambert has fulfilled that function with Ashton, Howard, Tudor, Staff, and many others.

(iii) BALLET IN BRITAIN

After spending the early war years in America, the Ballet Jooss, under the auspices of C.E.M.A., has made a re-appearance. *The Green Table* still remains the outstanding creation. Today, when its grim prophecy is actuality, it is even more impressive than formerly. It is a work that will endure. The new creations, however, reveal the limitations of movement self-imposed by Jooss. He tells a narrative admirably, but with too much literature at the expense of plastic art. The elaborate costumes used call out for scenery to complete the ballet, and there has been no advance in the use of music. One asks oneself if this obviously sincere artist, creator of a masterpiece and many works of rare charm such as *Ball in Old Vienna,* with his wonderfully precise company, will go much farther along the path he has chosen. At present he is sitting on a fence between ballet proper and the spoken drama of a *théâtre des quinze.* It seems as if either he must take in scenery, an orchestra, and a richer repertoire of movement, or add speech to a form of theatre that tends to become arid. I write with diffidence, and deliberately so, because Jooss has proved himself in the past and has trained a superb team. If only a personality would emerge from that team, even at the risk of disturbing what is a limited but almost monotonous level of perfection!

Since the main text of this book was written, another large-scale company has been formed—The International Ballet. It has shown hospitality to the classics and has produced such experimental works as *Everyman* and *Twelfth Night.* Experiment deserves encouragement, but the first subject would seem out of place in the ballet medium, especially wedded to the music of Richard Strauss, and the second requires the language of Shakespeare to make it anything more than a trivial tale with too many twists and turns to be easily told in ballet.

It is a remarkable fact that in spite of war a company on such a scale could have been formed and could have built up an important repertoire. It shows the extra-ordinary demand for ballet today. Escapism? Partly, but *re*-creation would be an apter word.

(iv) THE RUSSIAN COMPANIES

These familiar and welcome visitors to pre-war England have found a home in America. They have undergone so many splits and changes that it would require a weekly edition of any book to keep pace with them. The temptations of Hollywood and musical comedy have thinned the ranks of the well-known dancers; others, mainly Americans, have taken their places, till Russian Ballet, as we know it, has become Russo-American Ballet, which may in time bring interesting results. America, with its rich mixed cultures, is a fine field for ballet, if enthusiasm can be checked by a respect for tradition. Our own Markova and Dolin have remained magnificently true to their traditions, and no classical dancer since Pavlova has gained such a position as Markova. Long may the purity of her art flourish.

Two choreographers known to us here as beginners have made outstanding reputations: Anthony Tudor and Agnes de Mille; the famous Russians seem to have added little to theirs. This and the increasingly American composition of the companies points to the end of the *émigré ballet russe* that we have known since the days of Diaghileff, and that gave us both the love and the practice of the art.

An epoch ended with the death in America (1943) of Fokine. He was the first modernist in ballet, though we think of him mistakenly as a classicist. He remains the greatest. In spite of the hundreds of productions since 1914, neither Fokine himself nor anyone else has equalled *Les Sylphides, Le Spectre de la Rose, Prince Igor, Scheherazade, Petrouchka, The Firebird,* with the exception of Fokine's own later inspiration, *L'Épreuve d'Amour.* It is fitting that he should have died after a triumphant success, *Bluebeard,* yet to be seen in England. Gradually these works will lose their style and the creator's many master touches. To have seen them produced by him, and to have watched him at work, building up his effects, was a great privilege. Apart from his works, Fokine's principles must be remembered for all time. They are the foundation upon which all the future must be built. If he is forgotten, as was Noverre until he came along, ballet will return once again to the music-hall, as an interlude between the red-nosed comic and the performing seals.

(v) BEHIND THE SCENES

There are many encouraging things unknown to the general public going on behind the scenes in the world of ballet. There is the Royal Academy of Dancing to ensure that teaching retains its integrity, to maintain a general high standard from which the exceptional can come. There are enthusiastic ballet clubs all over the country, forming audiences aware of the finer points of taste and technique, and avoiding the pitfalls of uncritical adulation. There is the Production Club sponsored by the Royal Academy, a potentially great influence that will bring a practice of the art as distinct from the technique within reach of thousands of students and will so form a choreographic nursery. The conception of this club and the scope on which it is planned for peace-time development should make it of major importance.

And these influences are not only at work in the Mother Country. The Royal Academy is at work all over the Empire; its examinations have continued throughout the war. The inspirer of its activities is Adeline Genée, continuing her great career for the benefit of the country that first acclaimed her, seconded by P. J. S. Richardson, editor of the *Dancing Times* and joint founder of the Camargo Society; and, for the Production Club, that fine artist Ursula Moreton.

In Australia the split in Russian ballet has proved of great benefit, leaving behind Helen Kirsova and Édouard Borovansky, who have formed their own Australian companies, an important event in an essentially musical and artistic community that breeds such magnificent physical specimens.

Never has the outlook for creative ballet in Britain and the Commonwealth seemed brighter; the method has been established, the public is there, a new body, C.E.M.A.,[1] holds a watching brief for the State and forms the ideal British compromise, halfway between State control and indifference. In ten years' time the chapter on the British effort in this work will have grown beyond all recognition.

[1] Now the Arts Council of Great Britain.

Illustrated Glossary of some Common Terms

Adagio signifies the " high spot " of the ballet, when the *ballerina,* assisted by her partner, displays her grace

and virtuosity. It is the *aria* of opera. It is a slow movement stressing balance.

Arabesque. There are a number of different *arabesques.* Basically it is the position of the body on one leg with the other extended behind, one arm in front and the other behind, forming the longest line that can be made from finger-tips to toes. The graceful, sweeping line along the back contrasts with, and is accentuated by, the angle formed by the legs. (See illustration above.)

Attack. The method of presentation, the deliberation behind the performance of the steps.

Attitude. Carlo Blasis finished a pirouette in the pose of Gian Bologna's famous Mercury. There are a number of possible attitudes. (See illustration below.)

Balletomane is a word first used in Russia to signify the man who never missed a single performance, sitting in the front-row seats, which were almost impossible to obtain without good fortune or influence, being often handed down from father to son. The *balletomane* was usually a staunch conservative and a fierce partisan. After the performance he would adjourn to a café, meet the dancers, and discuss the ballets until the early hours. He was as mad as anyone with a hobby, but well-informed, a mine of history and tradition, and a connoisseur of technique.

Today the word might be translated by " ballet fan." Anyone who visits the ballet a few times and knows a dancer calls himself a *balletomane*. There are also near-lunatics with all the enthusiasm but little of the knowledge of the Russian *balletomane,* who cause a certain amount of damage and a great deal of merriment. The present writer was responsible for loosing the word on the English language and for coining *balletomania* to describe the particular disease, and has suffered for it in many ways, but has no wish to be cured.

Barre. A rod running round the walls of a dance-studio which the pupils hold during their first exercises and while they are being placed. It steadies them, taking the place of the partner's hand.

Centre Practice. The second half of the ballet class, in which the *barre* is not used for support.

Divertissement. An entertainment made up of a series of disconnected dances, usually a hopeless muddle; cf. *suit de danses.*

Elevation. Dancing in the air, *la grâce sautée,* as opposed to *terre-à-terre* dancing. Elevation came in with the shortening of the skirts. The importance is not merely the height reached—this must depend on the time allowed by the music—but the gentleness of the landing. A loud thud will destroy all illusion of flying.

Enchaînement is the sequence of steps; a phrase in the poem that is a dance.

Entrechat. A jump during which the feet change their

ing: it is entirely inaccurate. Ballet dancing existed before the use of points, and exists without their use.

The foot can be *à terre* (on the ground), *à quart* (heel slightly off the ground), *sur la demi-pointe, à trois quarts*.

Tour en l'Air. A complete aerial turn of the body.

Index

202

Index

Index

Index

Music in England

ERIC BLOM

A107

A discussion of English musical life from the beginnings to the present day, setting the scene in which music has unfolded itself not only through the activities of composers, but also those of performers, scholars, and institutions.

"The best thing of its kind that has been done in this country for many a year. In a most readable form, he has compressed a vast amount of information into the two hundred pages at his disposal. The reader Mr. Blom has in mind is the plain man wishing to become better acquainted with what English musicians have done in the past, what they are doing now, and what may, perhaps, lie in the future ; and there is no doubt that he has accomplished his task with supreme success."—*Musical Opinion.*

"Mr. Blom tells his long story adroitly and with a surprising amount of detail considering the need for compression. He makes many a good point, bringing out the essential character of each period as it passes without checking the flow of the main current of events. . . . His estimates of composers are essentially sound."— *Times Literary Supplement.*

A Survey of Russian Music

M. D. CALVOCORESSI

A137

A brief but complete history of the development of music in Russia from its beginnings in folk song and primitive opera to the present time. The work of every Russian composer, famous or comparatively little known, is discussed and described: special attention is paid to the local and national schools of various parts of what is now the U.S.S.R., to the work of modern Soviet composers, and to composers of Russian origin who are now working outside their native country.

PELICAN BOOKS

Recent Titles in Pelican Books

Recent and Forthcoming Penguins